Winning Chess ♛ Tournaments for Juniors

Robert M. Snyder
**National Chess Master and
Director of Chess for Juniors**

**Random House
Puzzles & Games**

Please address inquiries about electronic licensing of reference products, for use on a
network or in software or on CD-ROM, to the Subsidiary Rights Department, Random House
Information Group, fax 212-940-7352.

This book is available for special discounts for bulk purchases for sales promotions or
premiums. Special editions, including personalized covers, excerpts of existing books, and
corporate imprints, can be created in large quantities for special needs. For more
information, write to Special Markets/ Premium Sales, 1745 Broadway, MD 6-2, New York,
NY, 10019 or e-mail *specialmarkets@randomhouse.com*.

Visit the Random House Puzzles & Games Web site: www.puzzlesatrandom.com

Typeset and printed in the United States of America.

Library of Congress Cataloging-in-Publication Data is available.

First Edition
0 9 8 7 6 5 4 3 2 1
ISBN: 0-8129-3635-3

Acknowledgments

Thanks are due to Calvin Olson for his assistance in proofreading and reviewing the original manuscript. His assistance as a consultant in the areas of chess literature, psychology, and tournament direction was invaluable.

Introduction

After writing *Chess for Juniors* and *Unbeatable Chess Lessons for Juniors* I completed a comprehensive series of formal lessons that would take the beginner to an advanced level. These books provide students with a great deal of theoretical knowledge and form the basis for a book on the practical application of this knowledge.

Because of the consistent and overwhelming success of my individual students at the National Scholastic Championships I was urged to write a book covering what these players did and how they prepared for tournaments. A short biography with detailed analysis of games of some these champions is included.

Winning Chess Tournaments for Juniors, though directed at the intermediate and advanced level scholastic player, is a book for any player who knows the basics, regardless of age. Players who have read or understand the material covered in *Chess for Juniors* or who have a

National Chess Rating between 700 and 2000 will find this book to be invaluable. Chess teachers and coaches will also find this book to be a valuable resource for training their players.

With the exception of a review of basic symbols used in this book, I excluded a primer covering basic rules or strategy, as these were all covered in *Chess for Juniors*. However, when I feel a review of a basic rule or strategic concept is important, it will be covered within the text of this book. When the names of the players at the beginning of a game are shown, the first player named, which is on the left, is playing White. Now, let's get into the first chapter.

Symbols Used In This Book

Symbol	Meaning
x	captures
+	check
++	checkmate
=	promoted to a
0-0	castles Kingside
0-0-0	castles Queenside
e.p.	en passant
?	weak move
??	very weak move (a blunder)
!	strong move
!!	very strong move

Contents

What It Takes to Be a Successful Tournament Competitor

I am always being asked, *"How good can I get?"* How good you can get depends on how much natural talent you have and what you do to improve your game. The good news is that a student with little talent can still become a good player by putting in ample time and by doing things correctly. However, if you have talent and put in the time to study and practice you can become a great player! Becoming a national champion usually requires you to be dedicated, along with having self-discipline and a love for chess. This book is going to help you do things right by following the training methods used by my national scholastic champions. Three important aspects of chess training I will now discuss are: 1) finding a chess teacher, 2) reading chess books, and 3) playing chess.

FINDING A CHESS TEACHER

Most highly-rated scholastic players have a chess teacher. There is a good reason for this. An experienced chess teacher can guide you and provide you with a well-rounded study plan.

Private lessons are certainly the most efficient means of improving. However, for lower-rated players, group lessons can be more fun and affordable. Lessons with the instructor present are usually best for very young students who may require an element of entertainment during their lessons. However, for students who are well-focused and serious about improving their game, private lessons on the Internet can have advantages. Experienced Internet chess teachers will combine the graphic display on the Internet with a speakerphone to provide both visual and auditory communication with their students during lessons. Unlike giving a lesson in person, an Internet chess teacher can have instant access to preset positions, be able to immediately restore a previous position during analysis, use an extensive database for quick research, and use a computer program to assist with analysis. This can save an enormous amount of time during lessons!

It is also important for you to find the right teacher. A good youth chess teacher should have a good understanding of the game as well as the ability to make learning fun. Teaching and playing ability are two different skills. If you are paying a teacher for lessons, you should look for an instructor who has both good teaching skills and playing ability. As with any subject a teacher cannot effectively teach what he doesn't know.

Later in this book we will look at the national rating system. However, you should consider the following as a general guide for playing ability when looking for a paid instructor. An instructor with a rating of at least 1600 would be acceptable for beginners or players rated less than 1000. Once students get a rating over 1000, they should have an instructor rated at least three classes higher than themselves (600+ points above your rating). For students rated over 1800 the teacher should be rated at least two classes higher (400+ points). Once a student reaches a rating of 2100 or higher, the teacher will work more in the capacity of a trainer and should be rated at least one class higher (200+ rating points). Remember, these are only general guidelines if you are paying someone to teach you.

When looking for a teacher you should seriously consider the teacher's track record for producing good players. In evaluating teachers find out if they have produced any state or national champions and what the ratings are of their students. Check to see if they have published any articles or books containing instruction. Information on successful teachers can usually be found by doing research on the Internet.

Fees charged for private lessons can vary greatly, and affordability is usually an important factor in determining who your teacher will be and how often you receive lessons. Lower-rated, less experienced teachers might charge $10–$25 an hour for

A typical setup for an Internet chess lesson.

private lessons, whereas higher-rated, more experienced teachers may charge $25–$100 an hour. Most teachers will charge for their travel time and expense if the lessons are given at the student's home. Internet lessons have the advantage of not requiring either students or teachers to leave their homes!

Group lessons should cost considerably less. Group lessons with six or fewer students using a regular chess set are more efficient than larger groups, which require the use of a demonstration board. A demonstration board that has magnetic pieces or pieces inserted into slots is much slower to use than a regular chess set. However, demonstration boards are necessary and efficient when a teacher must reach a large group of students.

A demonstration board is used by teachers to reach a large number of students.

Ask your teacher if you can have your private lessons videotaped. Videotaping your private lessons will allow you to review the material covered whenever and as often as you want. The material is never lost, and you can build a library of your lessons. Taking notes can be helpful, but it takes up lesson time and is distracting.

A good teacher prepares lesson plans and develops a system. The main format of lessons should not consist of the teacher playing games against the student. This is not an efficient use of valuable lesson time. You should record your games against other players and bring them to your teacher for analysis.

How often you should take lessons depends on how much time and money you have. Certainly the more lessons you take the more you will learn. My average serious Internet student takes a one-hour lesson once a week. My group students attend a 90-minute class each week divided between 45 minutes of instruction and 45 minutes of practice. Some of my group students schedule an additional private lesson once a month to work on their individual strengths and weaknesses. Before making a long-

An ideal setup for a small group or private lessons using a standard chess set.

term commitment for group lessons be sure that the other students are close to your skill level. Before signing up for group instruction check to see how well the teacher maintains interest and control of the class.

Some chess teachers also provide coaching during tournaments. Having your teacher at major tournaments can be a major asset. A teacher can help you prepare for specific opponents, review your games, and be of assistance in many ways during the event.

An excellent way to receive additional instruction is to attend one or more of the many chess camps offered around the country. Camps vary greatly in quality based on their staff, organization, and the facilities at which they are held. When looking for a camp the main focus shouldn't be on how highly-rated the teachers are. Check into camps that have instructors with good teaching skills as well as high ratings. Some camps advertise that they have top notch Grandmasters. However, they are often hired based on their playing ability, not on teaching ability. A small camp where you spend more time with a limited number of instructors is usually better than a camp with many students and teachers. Often a large camp will not provide consistent individualized instruction. Also, look for camps that focus on instruction rather than only running several tournaments or having you play against the teachers.

Here are two contacts for information on qualified chess teachers and camps:

CHESS FOR JUNIORS
National Scholastic Internet Chess Training Center, Camps and
Colorado's Chess Club for Youth
www.chessforjuniors.com
Phone: 970-377-0011

INTERNATIONAL DIRECTORY OF CHESS TEACHERS
http://www.jaderiver.com/chess/teachers.html

READING BOOKS

I have heard more than once that there are more books written on chess than all other games in the world combined! Take advantage of this. I personally have more than 2,000 chess books in my private collection. Collecting chess books is fun, but can become expensive and space consuming. Luckily, you can have a well-rounded basic library consisting of about 20 books.

I will recommend some excellent books that you may consider as we get into different subject matters. I start here by recommending a basic book followed by a game collection book. If you have a rating under 1000 I would suggest you start by getting my book covering the basics, *Chess for Juniors* (New York: Random House, 1991). Then you should continue by reading the sequel, *Unbeatable Chess Lessons for Juniors* (New York: Random House, 2003). *Unbeatable Chess Lessons for Juniors* is recommended for players rated between 700 and 1800. It contains very detailed commentary with analysis of 24 instructive games. Another excellent book with detailed game commentary is *Logical Chess, Move by Move* by Irving Chernev, algebraic edition (London: Batsford, 1999). Both of these books have comments on every move.

There are thousands of books with game collections. A book I recommend for players rated over 1200 is *500 Master Games of Chess* by Tartakower & DuMont (New York: Dover, 1975). It contains excellent games with quality analysis. Going over complete games allows you to see the entire picture of what is happening that is often missed when starting from a set position.

PLAYING CHESS

Playing allows you to put the theories you have learned to a test. Keep in mind that you will usually learn more by playing against stronger players. Losing is part of the learning process. Everyone who plays loses games, including world champions.

Beginners should immediately start playing casual non-tournament games as soon as they learn the basic rules and have received some pointers on basic strategy. Casual games against friends and at your local chess club are extremely helpful for the beginning player.

Players should learn to condition themselves for tournaments by using the touch-move rule even in casual games. The touch-move rule states: 1) if you a touch a piece that can be moved, you must move it, 2) if you touch an opponent's piece that can be legally captured, you must capture it, and 3) once you take your hand off a piece after making a legal move, you cannot take it back. If it is obvious that a player didn't intend to move a touched piece or accidentally brushes a piece when making a move the touch-move rule doesn't apply. An example of this would be if a piece is accidentally knocked over, picked up, and replaced on the square it was on. In that event the player wouldn't be required to move the piece. However, if you notice that a piece is not well centered on a square and want to adjust it, you should say *"adjust"* before touching it; this avoids the problem of the opponent invoking the touch-move rule.

A special application of the touch-move rule is involved in castling. Castling involves moving two pieces that together constitute a single move. The rule is that the King is moved two spaces in the direction that castling is to take place and the Rook is placed on the other side of the King. Although current USCF (United States Chess Federation) rules do not penalize a player for touching the Rook first, players should follow the correct procedure of moving the King first and then the Rook. The reason for this is that in all international competitions, and in all other countries, the FIDE (International Chess Federation) rules are enforced. Under FIDE rules, if you touch the Rook first then castling is not allowed and you must move the Rook. A harsh penalty, but those are the rules.

Once beginners have a solid knowledge of the rules, understand basic strategy, know how to record their moves and use a chess clock, they are ready to play in their first nationally-rated chess tournament. Many scholastic tournaments have a special section for lower-rated players. For psychological reasons it is usually best for most scholastic players to begin playing in scholastic tournaments instead of adult tournaments. When my students get national ratings over 1200 I recommend that they also start playing in adult tournaments. With the exception of state and national scholastic championships most scholastic tournaments don't provide a high level of competition for players rated over 1400.

Playing in nationally-rated tournaments is the best form of practice. It is here that players will take their game seriously and try their best to win. It is best to use a score book rather than individual score sheets. Using a score book keeps the games together in chronological order and is more difficult to lose than an individual score sheet. Since tournament games are recorded, after a game is over it is a good idea to review the game with your opponent to find out what ideas he was considering during the game. If possible, have your games analyzed by your chess teacher.

In order to play in nationally-rated tournaments you must be a member of the *United States Chess Federation (USCF)*. You may contact them at

UNITED STATES CHESS FEDERATION
www.uschess.org
Phone: 845-562-8350

You may also want to get a free copy of *A Guide to Scholastic Chess* from the USCF. If you don't have a chess club at your school this book will help you with the information you need to get one started. It also contains a lot of other useful information for scholastic players and coaches.

The Internet provides students anywhere in the world with an opportunity to play chess whenever they want. Besides receiving lessons online you can play chess any time from the convenience of your own home. Most of my serious students practice regularly on the *Internet Chess Club (ICC)*. You may contact ICC at

INTERNET CHESS CLUB
www.chessclub.com
Phone: 412-521-5553

Due to the high quality of service that the ICC provides and the ease of finding opponents of any playing ability, it is well worth the small annual membership fee charged. They offer a discount for scholastic players and provide a central meeting ground for students to come together to play and socialize. ICC also runs online tournaments. Every three months I run a scholastic tournament on ICC (while on ICC type in FINGER CFJ-TOURN for details). The USCF also offers a free online service for its members.

Getting a chess-playing program for your computer is an excellent idea. Not only do you have an opponent available 24 hours a day, you have instant access to large databases for study. One of the strongest and most sophisticated programs is *Fritz*. Information on this program, which was developed in Germany, is available at *www.chessbase.com*. Another program, which is very popular and widely distributed in stores, is *Chessmaster*. Both of these programs are constantly being upgraded with newer versions.

Dedicated chess computers with "stand-up" pieces can be very strong, and their portability makes them convenient for travel. Since they have multiple settings for different playing abilities, it is a good idea to get a dedicated chess computer with a strong program—it avoids having to buy another computer as you improve.

Playing speed chess (also sometimes called blitz or five-minute chess) can be helpful if kept in moderation. Besides being fun it is a great way to test your openings and sharpen your tactical skills. Speed chess uses a chess clock, usually giving each player a total of one to ten minutes of thinking time. It requires the players to make quick and sometimes superficial judgments to avoid losing on time. I usually recommend that my students don't play any faster than having three minutes thinking time on each side. Playing faster than that becomes more of a contest of how fast you can move the pieces, and the quality of the moves becomes less important. The drawback of playing too much speed chess is that students may become so geared to moving fast that they might have difficulty slowing down to the pace of a regular tournament game. This can lead to losses when you don't take the time to analyze the opponent's threats. Mental discipline is required to slow down when quickly switching from speed chess to playing a slow tournament game. Therefore, playing speed chess just before a regular tournament game is not recommended. Most sanctioned speed chess tournaments require players to use touch-move rules and to "punch the clock with the same hand that moves the piece." When playing speed chess for fun you should condition yourself to those same rules to make them instinctive.

If you are an advanced player you may enjoy the challenge of giving simultaneous exhibitions. This is where you play against many other players at the same time. This also gives less experienced players an opportunity to play against a strong player.

There are two items of training that players should be aware of when preparing for tournaments: pattern recognition and conditioning (both physical and mental). Pattern recognition is the perception of similar themes involving the interaction of pieces on the board. These same patterns can occur in different positions. Therefore pattern recognition, which will be studied in detail later in this book, is critical when it comes

Twelve-year-old Zachary Bekkedahl plays against seven other students simultaneously at the Chess For Juniors Club.

to improving your game. Anything that distorts the perception of patterns should be avoided.

DISTORTING PATTERN RECOGNITION

Playing variations of chess that change some of the rules and/or the way the pieces move can be harmful. A couple of examples are Bughouse or Suicide (also sometimes called Give Away chess). They distort pattern recognition because of their use of changes to the game. A controlled scientific study involving Bughouse was made in Germany, which verified that it has a detrimental effect on chess-playing ability.

Serious chess students want to train their mind to focus on the types of patterns that will occur in their tournament games. Therefore, the time spent on Bughouse chess is distracting and gears the mind to analyze patterns that cannot be used in standard chess. While some students are playing in the Bughouse tournaments at the national championships, my students are either resting or studying standard chess.

TOURNAMENT CONDITIONING

As in other sports, chess coaches want their players to be in the best possible condition. This may require you to sacrifice some of the fun things you do on non-chess trips. However, you will have more fun in the end by having better results in tournaments! Here I will go over some recommendations for players to follow before and during tournaments.

If you are traveling to a major tournament try to arrive at least a day before and depart the day after the event. Players need time to rest and get adjusted after a long trip, especially when traveling across one or more time zones. It can be very stressful trying to rush to get to an airport on time if the flight is scheduled to leave on the same day the tournament begins or ends. Also, players often will miss the awards ceremony, a major disappointment if either a player or a team is due to receive a prize.

If you are going to do any extracurricular activities on a trip to a tournament, try and schedule these activities after the tournament instead of before. I always fly instead of drive when taking my students to an event that would require more than an eight-hour drive. Long drives or excessively long flights can wear down a player before the tournament even begins. When possible I try to get a direct flight for my group.

It is important to get good sleep each night during the tournament. Players should go to bed early enough to get a sufficient amount of sleep. You need to consider any changes due to traveling through time zones. It is usually impossible to go to sleep at a normal time on the first night if you have traveled east through two or three time zones. Therefore, if you have traveled east through times zones, add some time before going to bed. If you have traveled west through time zones subtract time. Sometimes the period between the ending of the last round and the beginning of the first morning round is minimal. Therefore, instead of getting up early to go out for a formal breakfast, I sometimes allow the players to sleep in and then have a continental breakfast. It is important to eat something before your first round in the morning.

Players should be well-rested before rounds. Avoid excessive physical activity just before a round. Going swimming before rounds should be avoided because of chlorine getting in your eyes. Playing video games on chess trips should be avoided. It causes eyestrain and fatigue. Video games also distract your focus from chess. I have also seen a player with a headset listening to music during his round while chewing gum and standing on his chair! Leave the headset and gum at home and sit down with your buttocks on the chair. This will certainly help you focus on your game and increase your chances of winning.

You should avoid eating a big meal just before a round. Try to finish eating at least 45 minutes to an hour before your round starts. Avoid eating a lot of foods with high sugar content or having drinks with caffeine. You should have enough liquids in your system to avoid dehydration. Sometimes having a cup of water near your board during a tournament game is a good idea. However, don't become so waterlogged that you are forced to be making constant trips to the restroom while you are playing!

It is also very important to be in good physical shape. A major problem that often occurs toward the end of a long game or tournament is fatigue. There can be a lot of stress during a tournament, and a player can easily become worn down. Making sure that you are in good physical shape is the best way to fight against fatigue.

Many years ago I took one of my very talented elementary students to the National Elementary School and National Junior High School Championships when they were held on two consecutive weekends. On the second weekend he won his first five games in a row and was tied for first place. About halfway through his sixth round he went brain dead and simply couldn't think. He explained after the game was over that he became so fatigued that he couldn't concentrate. He went on to lose his next round as well. The major problem was that he wasn't in good physical shape. He wasn't involved in any sports or activities outside of chess. I highly recommend that you have at least one other sport or activity that keeps you in good physical shape. I was involved with tennis and dirt biking and even reached the level of Black Belt in karate.

During a tournament game, if you have been sitting for a long period and have plenty of time on your chess clock you may want to get up, stretch, and perhaps even take a short walk. This helps in avoiding both mental and physical fatigue from sitting too long. However, on your walk don't start analyzing your friends' games. Taking a quick glance at them and analyzing them are two different things. Maintain focus on your own game!

There will be many more recommendations, such as items that pertain to tournament rules, psychology, and how and what to study that will be covered later in this book.

How Tournaments Work and How to Use Rules to Your Favor

It is important to know how tournaments are run and have a detailed knowledge of tournament rules and how to apply them. Many players miss opportunities because they don't understand a rule or their rights. During a tournament game parents and coaches are not allowed to make claims on your behalf. Therefore, you are responsible for knowing the rules and making claims. Players need to be their own attorney! In ways such as this chess helps prepare you for life.

Every tournament competitor should own a copy of *Official Rules of Chess*, 5th edition (New York: Random House, 2003). The *Official Rules of Chess* covers in great detail all of the rules, the national rating system, and how tournaments are run. In this book we will focus on what is most important for you to know as a player from a practical point of view.

There are basically two different systems used to run nationally-rated tournaments. The most common, and the main focus of this chapter, is the Swiss system tournament. Swiss system tournaments are popular because they are the most effective type of tournament when a large number of players are competing in a short period of time, whereas Round-Robin tournaments typically have each player play one game against everyone else in a section. The Round-Robin is an excellent system if there are a very small number of players in the tournament or if you have a tournament composed of several small sections.

THE SWISS SYSTEM TOURNAMENT

In a Swiss system tournament there are a set number of rounds (most scholastic tournaments have between four and nine rounds and usually last from one to three days). Players are paired against an opponent in each round with all rounds after the first taking into consideration the players' current scores, ratings, and the number of times they have played White or Black. A player can never play the same opponent more than one time in the same tournament.

Players receive one point for a win, half a point for a draw, and zero points for a loss. The points accumulate as you play each round, and at the end of the tournament the player with the most points wins first place, the player with the second most points wins second place, and so on. There are usually ties so there are numerous tiebreak systems used to determine winners. We will discuss tiebreak systems later.

In the first round players are seeded based on their national chess ratings, with the top-rated player listed as number one, the second highest rated player listed as number two, and so on. The boards are numbered, and in the first round the highest rated player will play at board number one. In a standard Swiss system tournament the top half of the players are paired against the bottom half. To give you an example of how this works let's say there are eight players in a tournament. Player number one is paired against player number five, player number two against player number six, number three against seven and number four against number eight. Before the first round is paired either a coin is tossed or a computer is used to make a random selection to determine which player gets the White pieces on the first board. If the top player is White in the first round, the second highest player gets Black, the third highest rated player gets White with the alternation of colors continuing in that manner.

After the first round, players with the same scores are paired. Within that score group the players are lined up by rating and then the top half of the players are paired against the bottom half. Adjustments are made to attempt to allow players to play White and Black an equal number of times. For example, if a player after three rounds has played White twice and Black once he will usually play Black in the fourth round. If there is an odd number of players in a score group, the lowest-rated player in the group is paired with the highest-rated player in the next lower score group.

In theory there should be only one winner with a perfect score in a Swiss system tournament. However, if there are too many players and not enough rounds it is possible to have more than one player with a perfect score. If there are 16 players in a four round tournament there can be only one perfect score (32 players with five rounds, 64 players with six rounds, 128 players with seven rounds, and 256 players for eight rounds).

If there are a lot more players than there should be for the set number of rounds some tournaments will use accelerated pairings. This variation of the Swiss system will divide the pairings into two groups, the top half and the bottom half, and then make the pairings within the two groups. Using our example of a tournament with eight players, the players will be paired in quarters. On the top half player number one is paired against player number three and number two is paired against number four. On the bottom half player number five will play player number seven and number six will play number eight.

If the number of players in a tournament is odd, then one player must sit out each round. That player is given a *"bye,"* which counts as a full point for scoring purposes. Some tournaments will allow a player to request a *"bye"* if they are unable to play in one or more rounds. In this case the player receives only half a point (the same as a draw). The number of *"byes"* that can be requested may vary from one tournament to another. Most tournaments do not allow for a player to request a *"bye"* for the last round. My students will often request a *"bye"* if they must miss part of the tournament due to another commitment.

At the beginning of each round pairing sheets are posted providing you with information showing you who you will be playing, what board number you are on, and what color you will be playing. There is a number at each board. In a major tournament you should arrive early to have enough time to find your board. Be sure you have the right board number and color when you sit down! It is very important that when your game is over you correctly report your result. In most major national and state championships a reporting form is left at each board before the round starts. Please be sure that you and your opponent correctly mark down the result of your game and sign it. Sometimes in smaller tournaments, the players will report their results by marking them down on the pairing sheet. Once again be sure that both you and your opponent correctly mark down your score. If a player didn't show up for a round and you win by default you should indicate this by writing the word "forfeit." Do not rely on your opponent to report the result of the game properly. *To avoid any possible errors, make sure you report the result yourself!*

READING A WALL CHART

A wall chart is used to provide information about all of the players and show how they are doing in the tournament. It is important for you to learn how to read a wall chart. The following is an example of a wall chart from an actual tournament, which shows the results of a four-round tournament.

The following numbers explain the circled numbers on the wall chart:

1) Round Number—All of the information and results of the first round are located vertically below on this column.

2) Player's Number—All players are assigned a number based on their national ratings. The higher the rating the lower their player number is.

3) Player's Name—Zachary Bekkedahl, being the highest-rated player, was seeded as number one. *Verify that your name is spelled correctly.*

4) Player's National Rating—Zachary has a national chess rating of 1417. *Verify that your rating is correct.*

5) Player's USCF Identification—All players, after joining the USCF, are given a permanent ID number. It is very important to *verify that this number is correct.*

6) Player's Color (W = White, B = Black)—Zachary played White in the first round.

7) Player's Opponent—Zachary played against player number 8, Alex Tallant, in the first round.

8) Player's Cumulative Score—The total number of points that a player has is shown. Zachary won his first round and has one point.

9) Player's Cumulative Score After Four Rounds—Zachary won all four of his games and got four points.

10) Unplayed Game—Paul Baxter didn't play his third (and fourth) round.

11) Bye—A one-point bye was given to Stephen Meyer in the first round.

12) Unrated—Reece Lindholm didn't have a rating.

13) No ID Number—Reece Lindholm just recently joined the USCF and hadn't been assigned an ID number yet.

CHESS FOR JUNIORS JAN 2003 SCHOLASTIC

Cross Table

Name/Rtng/ID#/Team/State/Gr/rd1	rd2	rd3	rd4
1 Bekkedahl, Zachary..........W 8	B 5	W 4	B 3
1417 12805139 1.0	2.0	3.0	4.0
2 Baxter, Paul...............B 9	W 7	----	----
1152 12876351 1.0	2.0	2.0	2.0
3 Chen, Peter H.............W 10	B 13	W 5	W 1
1094 12840635 1.0	2.0	3.0	3.0
4 Dickinson, Ethan..........B 11	W 14	B 1	W 7
1015 12850109 1.0	2.0	2.0	2.5
5 Meyer, Stephen K..........bye	W 1	B 3	B 12
987 12854828 1.0	1.0	1.0	2.0
6 Binder, Matt.............B 14	W 8	W 11	B 15
971 12875132 0.0	0.0	0.0	1.0
7 Boisdore, Matthew.........W 15	B 2	W 13	B 4
767 12764918 1.0	1.0	2.0	2.5
8 Tallant, Alex.............B 1	B 6	W 15	W 10
657 12859053 0.0	1.0	2.0	3.0
9 Stapleton, Michelle........W 2	B 15	B 14	W 11
591 12871138 0.0	0.0	1.0	2.0
10 Stapleton, Carla...........B 3	B 11	W 12	B 8
320 12871139 0.0	1.0	1.5	1.5
11 Carmichael, Ian R..........W 4	W 10	B 6	B 9
315 12876253 0.0	0.0	1.0	1.0
12 McCormick, Nate.............W 13	bye	B 10	W 5
100 12881237 0.0	1.0	1.5	1.5
13 Lindholm, Reece............B 12	W 3	B 7	W 14
unr. NEW 1.0	1.0	1.0	2.0
14 Johnson, Erik M............W 6	B 4	W 9	B 13
unr. NEW 1.0	1.0	1.0	1.0
15 Sorenson, Erik.............B 7	W 9	B 8	W 6
unr. NEW 0.0	1.0	1.0	1.0

Sample wall chart.

BREAKING TIES

At the end of a tournament there are numerous tie-breaking systems that can be used when players end up with the same number of points. Because it is very time consuming to have players with tie scores playing more games ("play-offs") to determine a winner, this is rarely done in Swiss system tournaments. We will now briefly discuss a few of the most commonly used systems to break ties.

The *"Solkoff"* tie breaking system adds up the final scores of all of your opponents. The idea is that the player who played against stronger opponents should win on the tie breaks. There are adjustments made for games that aren't played. For example if the player played against an opponent who had a bye, forfeit, or unplayed games (in the case of withdrawal) such games are each counted as a half-point. Unplayed games of a player involved in a tie are also adjusted this way, with the exception of a forfeit win being counted as zero.

The *"Modified Median"* tie-breaking system is the same as the *Solkoff* except all of the players with even scores (i.e., have 2.5 points in a five-round tournament or 3 points in a six-round tournament) don't have their highest and lowest scoring opponents counted in the calculation. This is modified for players with minus scores (i.e., with 2 or fewer points in a five-round tournament) by discarding only the highest opponent from the calculation. For players with plus scores (i.e., with 3 or more points in a five-round tournament) only the lowest scoring opponent is discarded from the calculation.

For tournaments with nine or more rounds, players with even score ties have the top two and bottom two scoring players discarded from the calculation, players with minus score ties have only the highest two scoring players discarded and players with plus score ties have only the bottom two scoring players discarded.

The *"Cumulative"* tie-breaking system adds up the running scores of the players involved in the tie break for each round. This is quick and easy to calculate. For example you will note that there were two players tied with three points on the tournament wall chart used in this book. Peter Chen, player number 3, won his first three and lost his final round game, shown as 1, 2, 3, and 3 on the chart. His score using the *"Cumulative"* system was 9. Alex Tallant, player number 8, lost his first round and went on to win his next three rounds, shown as 0, 1, 2, and 3. His score was 6. Players are rewarded for winning early rounds using this system.

In the tournament shown on the wall chart, the *"Solkoff"* system was used as the first tie break with the *"Cumulative"* system used to break any ties that still resulted after the use of the first tie-breaking system. Trophies were awarded as follows, 1st place to Zachary Bekkedahl, 2nd place to Peter Chen, 3rd place to Alex Tallant, and 4th place to Matthew Boisdore. Scholastic tournaments will often have one or more prizes based on either rating or grade level. Reece Lindholm won the prize for being the top player rated under 700 on tie breaks over Michelle Stapleton. Note that Alex Tallant was rated under 700. However, since most tournaments *only allow a player to win one prize as an individual*, Tallant received the 3rd place trophy allowing Lindholm to receive a plaque for having the highest score by a player rated under 700.

Some tournaments also allow school or club teams to compete. Usually there must be a minimum of two players from the same school or club for them to be considered a team. There is usually no maximum number of players that can be on a team. However, usually the top four scores from the players on each team are added up; this means that any other scores by other players representing the team do not count.

THE USCF RATING SYSTEM

The United States Chess Federation (the governing body of chess in the United States) maintains and calculates the national rating system in this country. All players who complete in at least four rated games in a USCF rated tournament will receive a published rating. Ratings based on fewer than 25 games are considered *provisional* and use a formula to allow the ratings to quickly adjust to indicate a player's ability. A player is considered to have an *established* rating once 25 games have been played and rated.

Details containing the formulas used to calculate USCF ratings are at the USCF website and in the *Official Rules of Chess*. As a quick rule of thumb you gain more rating points for defeating a higher rated player (and lose fewer rating points for losing to a higher rated player) than defeating a lower rated player. You will also gain or lose rating points for drawing with players rated approximately 25 points or higher or lower than you. An established player will gain approximately 16 rating points for defeating a player with the same rating.

The USCF uses a scale that is divided into intervals of two hundred points to define the different classes of players. Although the system has been extended, the traditional method specified that any players under 1200 in rating were considered beginning level. Intermediate level players would then be from 1200 to 1800 (or 1900); players with a rating above that considered are strong players. The problem is that there is no clear-cut method of using ratings to define weak and strong players. This evaluation is based largely on adult players being included in the rating pool. For the placement of scholastic players into instructional group classes, I consider beginners as being below 700 in rating, intermediate players from 700 to 1099, and advanced players as 1100 and above. The level of a player at any given time is therefore described by the class. The following is the USCF scale for classes based on ratings:

CLASS OR TITLE	RATING
Senior Master	2400 and above
Master	2200 to 2399
Expert	2000 to 2199
Class A	1800 to 1999
Class B	1600 to 1799
Class C	1400 to 1599
Class D	1200 to 1399
Class E	under 1200*

(*The new system allows for classes down to the Class J level)

Ratings are often used to set up special prize categories at tournaments. Some sections in tournaments are limited to players rated under a certain rating or within a certain rating range. At some national scholastic championships junior varsity sections are set up allowing less experienced players, with lower ratings, to compete among themselves for prizes. This can make a trip to the national championships very worthwhile for a lower-rated player to gain experience while having a chance to win a prize. Top-rated players are often invited to certain tournaments based on their rating.

The average rated player in the country (taking adults into consideration) is approximately 1450. Most players as a result of playing in their first scholastic tournament start out with their rating between 300 and 1000. The USCF posts ratings on their Web site and mails rating supplements to USCF affiliate clubs around the country.

THE TOURNAMENT DIRECTOR

All nationally rated tournaments are required to have one or more *certified tournament directors*. The number of tournament directors and their required level of certification for a specific tournament is determined by guidelines set by the United States Chess Federation and is based on the size and importance of the event. Tournament directors are responsible for making pairings, enforcing rules, sending in rating reports, calculating and distributing prizes, making rulings, and handling problems and questions. In larger tournaments there is a "Chief" Tournament Director with assistant tournament directors under his command. In most cases computers are used to make pairings, print wall charts (also known as "crosstables"), and calculate the winners at the end of the tournament. This makes the tournament director's job much easier.

If any problems occur during one of your rounds you should immediately report it to a tournament director. Immediately stop your clock (we will discuss the use of chess clocks shortly). At most major scholastic tournaments you can summon a tournament director by raising your hand.

The tournament director may need to make a ruling on a claim that you make. In most cases the tournament director will make a correct ruling based on the rules. However, on occasion a tournament director may make an error. If you believe that the tournament director has made an incorrect ruling you have a right to appeal. If the tournament director who made the ruling isn't the Chief Tournament Director you may ask for the Chief Tournament Director to make a ruling. There are different levels of certified tournament directors and at major tournaments usually the first tournament director to assist isn't top dog!

It is important for you to show respect to the tournament director. However, you have a right to appeal when you feel that a ruling is not correct. In almost every case, if the Chief Tournament Director's ruling is the same it is a correct decision. Most tournament directors are friendly and will take the time to explain the reasoning behind their rulings. However, if you still do not agree, you have a right to insist on having a committee formed for a further investigation. If you have a coach on-site you should ask the tournament director to consult with your coach before asking for a committee or insisting on making a formal written appeal to the USCF. At that point if your coach agrees with the tournament director(s) you should accept the ruling and get back to focusing on the game.

In large tournaments there are usually several tournament directors. Whenever you make a claim or ask a tournament director a question during a game make a note of that name. For a first-time minor rule infraction a tournament director may just give a warning or impose a very small penalty. However, if the same problem occurs more than once a more severe penalty may be imposed for a second or third infraction. You will need the same tournament director to verify the earlier infraction. We will discuss infractions of the rules later on.

Always be sure to notify the tournament director if you cannot make a round so that you will not be paired and have an opponent waiting for you. This is also common courtesy.

THE CHESS CLOCK

I once heard a joke that went, "Before there were chess clocks it wasn't the person with the most brains who would win, it was the person with the most buttocks." Without a set amount of time for a player to think, either side could just sit there and not move. One story about a game played between two top players who were playing without a clock has both players sitting there for hours without a move being made. One of the players eventually looked at his opponent and said, "It's your move!" His opponent replied, "It is? I thought it was your move!"

In a tournament it is necessary to place a time limit on all of the games. A pairing for the next round cannot be made until all of the results have been posted. In the past it was common to *adjourn* games that were not finished by a certain time. However, nowadays most tournaments have a time control that will guarantee that all of the games are finished by a certain time. Most scholastic tournaments use a *sudden death* time control. The amount of time given varies from tournament to tournament. I use a sudden death time control where each player receives a total of 45 minutes thinking time. If a player uses up his 45 minutes before the game is finished the player forfeits the game. This guarantees that no game during the tournament will last longer than 90 minutes. Some scholastic tournaments give each side only 30 minutes. At most major national scholastic championships players usually have 90 to 120 minutes thinking time for each player.

It is the responsibility of the player to claim a win on time when the opponent runs out of time. If you don't claim your win your opponent may continue to play on until you make the claim. If your opponent runs out of time and then checkmates you before you make a claim, you lose!

In a sudden death time control some clocks allow for a *five-second time delay* so that when a player is just about to run out of time they will never lose on time if a move is always made within five seconds. When a clock is used that isn't set for time delay and there are two minutes or less left on the clock of a player, that player may claim *insufficient losing chances*. If you feel that you cannot avoid losing the game on time and the position is easily drawn or won, you may stop the clock and ask the tournament director to declare the game a draw because of insufficient losing chances. To make this claim when there is clearly no basis for it may result in having the tournament director subtract up to a minute from the clock of the player who made the claim.

Some tournaments require that the players make a set number of moves in the first hour and then have a sudden death time control for the second hour. In this case in order to claim a win on time during the first time control it is required for a player to have a reasonably accurate record of the moves in the game to prove how many moves were made. The rules define a reasonably accurate score sheet as one containing no more than three missing or incomplete move pairs. If for any reason you run out of time and your opponent starts filling in his score sheet before making his claim you should immediately declare that your time has run out and that your opponent doesn't have a complete score sheet. If necessary find a witness right away! If your opponent claims a win on time during a non–sudden death time control you should always challenge the accuracy of his score book with a tournament director present. It is very common for players to make numerous errors when recording moves.

There are basically two kinds of chess clocks. Both clocks in the picture have been set to give each player 45 minutes of thinking time. Digital clocks are more popular among students. They are more accurate than analog clocks. However, there are numerous makes and models of digital clocks and all have different formats for setting them. It is almost impossible for tournament directors to keep up with how to operate all of them. Therefore, it is especially important for you to have a good understanding of how your digital clock works before using it at a tournament.

You will note that there are two buttons at the top of each clock. After you make a move you *press* down the button on your side. This will stop your clock from running while starting your opponent's clock. Don't forget to press your clock after each move. If you forget, your opponent can just sit there until you remember or your time runs out.

Analog clocks are extremely easy to set. When setting an analog clock you set the first time control to expire at 6:00 so that both hands will not converge at the time control (this helps avoid any confusion). At the top of each clock you will see near the number 11 what is called a *"flag"* protruding down vertically. When the big hand gets past the number 11 it lifts the flag and when it reaches the number 12 the flag will fall. This will let you know exactly when a player's time runs out. Most digital clocks will flash or freeze the numbers when time is up.

When there are fewer than five minutes left on a clock in *"sudden death"* time control, both players are required to press the clock with the same hand that moves the piece and players do not need to record their moves. It is forbidden for either player to

A digital clock is shown on the left and an analog clock on the right.

pick up the clock at any point during the game. I recommend to my students that they should always press the clock with the same hand that moves the piece in order to make this procedure instinctive. It is a common mistake for players to not report it when their opponent doesn't press the clock with the hand that moves the piece when in time trouble. You have a right to report it and make an issue of it! Usually the tournament director will only give a warning to your opponent when it is reported. However, you should insist on a penalty when the same rule is constantly violated. You should point out if necessary that your opponent has already received a warning.

If an illegal move is made when there are fewer than five minutes left on a clock in sudden death time control the position before the illegal move is reinstated and two minutes are added to the clock of the player who didn't make the illegal move. However, once the player who made the illegal move has completed two moves the illegal move stands (also if either player resigns, is checkmated, or stalemated) and no time adjustment is made. This is certainly an incentive for a player not to declare that his opponent has made an illegal move if his opponent's illegal move was weak!

If both flags are down (both players having run out of time) during a sudden death time control the game results in a draw as soon as one of the players points it out. It isn't uncommon when both players are in serious time trouble that one of the players notices that both time allotments have expired! It is especially important to be alert and pay attention to what is happening with the clock if you are in time trouble.

There must be sufficient material on the board to be able to claim a win on time if your opponent's time expires. If one of the following exists when your opponent's time expires the game is a draw:

1) You only have your King left.
2) You only have a King and Bishop (or King and Knight) left and you don't have a forced win.
3) You only have a King and two Knights left and you don't have a forced win.

In most major scholastic tournaments standard chess sets are provided. It is rare for a tournament to provide chess clocks. If chess sets are not provided at the tournament and both sides have a standard chess set then the person playing the Black pieces decides which chess set to use. The same holds true for chess clocks. However, a digital clock always takes priority over an analog clock.

Also, in most major scholastic tournaments it is usually predetermined on which side of the board the clocks are placed. Otherwise, the player playing the Black pieces determines on which side of the board the clock will be placed. If the tournament doesn't provide sets and/or clocks or doesn't have a predetermined side of the board on which the clock is placed and if the Black player is late for the round, then the player of the White pieces can decide what equipment to use and on which side of the board the clock is placed.

RECORDING YOUR MOVES

In nationally rated tournaments both players are required to record all of the moves in the game with the exception being when there are fewer than five minutes left on the clock in sudden death time controls. Exceptions can also be made for players with physical handicaps or very young players who haven't developed writing skills. Writing down every move in a game may seem like a lot of hard work, but once you get used to it the practice becomes almost subconscious (like breathing—a piece of cake!).

In scholastic tournaments that I run it is required for students in Grade Two and above to record the moves in a score book to the best of their ability. I usually give students in Kindergarten or First Grade the option of recording their moves or using checkmarks in their score book. This makes it easier for very young players to start writing down real moves when they get older, and does not give younger players a significant advantage in time.

Recording your moves will allow you to review your game with your opponent and teacher after it is over. When I was young I was actually able to memorize every move of the first couple-hundred tournament games that I played! I was that serious about the game. However, I still recorded every tournament game and have most of them 35 years later.

Recording your moves is also like having an insurance policy. It helps to protect you by allowing you to show what the position was at any point of the game and if it was White or Black to move. Just how important this is cannot be overstated.

Imagine that your opponent reaches across the board when it is your turn to move, picks up your Queen and places it on the side of the board. It would be natural for you to start off by immediately going into a state of shock. Your instinct to reach across the board, grab your opponent by the collar of his shirt, and punch him must be resisted. Simply summon a tournament director, explain what happened, and hand him your score book. Your insurance policy has paid off. Without having a written record of the game the only evidence that you might have would be a witness who was watching your game. Don't count on that! If there are no witnesses other than you and your opponent, then the likely ruling would be that the position stands with you having no Queen. In most cases without a score sheet a claim is denied and, when it is the word of one player against another, what stands on the board stays on the board.

If players don't record their moves they lose their rights to claim a draw by repetition of position (the one exception being in time trouble when the game is observed by the tournament director), invoke the fifty-move rule, and claim a win on time (in a non–sudden death time control). They are unable to prove how many moves have been made by using their own score sheet as required.

If you make any mistakes in your score book you have the right to borrow your opponent's score book to make corrections, but only when it is your turn to move. If you are still unable to fix the problem then continue to write your moves down from that point on.

You or your opponent may write down your move before or after the move is made. Some teachers recommend that you write your move down before making your move and then think about it some more. For an impulsive player who typically moves too quickly this advice may be good. However, the disadvantage of writing your move down before making a move is that you will be writing both your own and your opponent's move while your clock is running. Also, unless you hide the move after you write it down this would allow your opponent to see the move and start thinking about what to do against it. If you decide on another move after writing it down you must take the time to scratch it out and write down another move. This would likely be a psychological boost for your opponent; you will have shown your opponent uncertainty in knowing what you are doing. We will discuss more on psychology in chess later in this book.

THE DRAWN GAME

There are numerous ways that a game can end in a draw, a situation where there is no winner and no loser. In tournaments a half-point is given to both the players when a game results in a draw. In most cases a half-point will make a major difference in the standings and awards given at tournaments. It isn't uncommon in scholastic tournaments for a game to end in a draw where one of the players should have easily won. This is one reason that I tell my students not to resign even when things seem hopelessly lost. Knowing the rules well may help save you from losing a game! I will now cover most of the possible types of draws. Some draws related to the use of the clock have already been covered.

A *"stalemate"* is the best-known draw among beginners who have not been formally introduced to chess. Unfortunately, laymen tend to use this as a generic term for all draws when it applies only to one of many ways that a game can be drawn. A stalemate occurs when the King of the player whose turn it is to move is not in check and there is no legal move that can be made with the King or any other piece.

Usually the side that gets stalemated has few if any pieces (other than the King) left on the board.

Stalemates occur most commonly during games played by beginners. One side will get far ahead and will accidentally stalemate his opponent. However, I have seen over-confidence and carelessness in games where even a strong player will accidentally have his game result in a draw because of a stalemate. We will now take a look at some instructive examples of ways stalemate is used to save what would otherwise be a hopeless situation. See if you can find White's best move in Diagram 1, below.

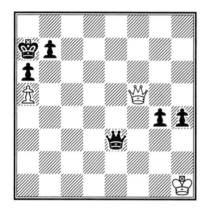

Diagram 1. Pilnik versus Reshevsky, US Championship, 1942. White to move and draw.

In Diagram 1, Black was three Pawns ahead and confident of an easy victory. It certainly came as a shock to Black when White played **1 Qf2!** pinning Black's Queen to his King. To avoid losing his Queen, Black was forced to stalemate White with **1...Qxf2**.

In Diagram 2, we have a position taken from one of my games when I was a scholastic player. I was dead lost throughout much of the game but stubbornly played on instead of resigning. I knew exactly what kind of position I needed in order to swindle my opponent out of his win!

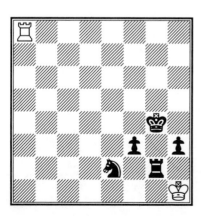

Diagram 2. White to move and draw.

I placed my King in the corner where he had no place to move. Black was threatening 1...Ng3++. With only my Rook able to move I continued with **1 Rg8+ Kf5 2 Rf8+ Kg6 3 Rg8+ Kf7**. My opponent didn't expect my next move! I played **4 Rf8+!**. My opponent stood up out of his chair and stared at the position for a minute realizing that if he took my Rook with 4...Kxf8 it would be stalemate! Therefore, he thought he came up with a good plan and the game continued after 4 Rf8+ with **4...Kg6 5 Rg8+ Kf5 6 Rf8+ Kg4 7 Rg8+ Kh4 8 Rh8+ Kg3 9 Rxh3+!** (my opponent was hoping for 9 Rg8+ when he could have successfully hidden his King with 9...Kf2) **Kf2** (once again taking the Rook with 9...Kxh3 would be stalemate) **10 Rxf3+!**. Black now must capture White's Rook or lose his own Rook, so the game ended in stalemate after **10...Kxf3**. If Black tried to hide by 1 Rg8+ Kf4 2 Rf8+ Ke3 (or Kg3) with the idea of going to f2, then 3 Rxf3+ with the same idea of continuing to check the King, because if the Rook is captured without an escape square for the White King, it is an automatic stalemate.

In Diagram 3, stalemate is once again used as the theme to obtain a draw in what would otherwise be a hopelessly lost game. See if you can find White's moves that force a draw.

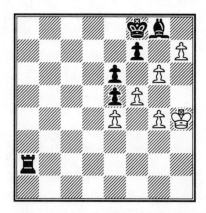

Diagram 3. White to move and draw.

Here is the solution to the problem in Diagram 3: **1 h8=Q Rh2+** (Black is forced to use a skewer to win White's Queen, otherwise he will lose) **2 Kg5 Rxh8 3 g7+!** (White gives up a Pawn to force Black to take away squares that White's King can move to—this is in the theme of setting up a stalemate) **Kxg7 4 f6+ Kh7** (if 4...Kf8 then Black has stalemated White) **5 Kh5**. Amazing! Black is the one stalemated.

Another common way a player may avoid losing is by claiming a draw by *repetition of position*. If the exact same position appears, or is about to appear on the next move, for at least the third time, with the same player to move, then the player who has the move may claim a draw. In either of these cases the position is considered to be the same if all of the pieces of the same color are on the same squares and all of the pieces have the same legal moves available to them. This includes being able to castle or capture a Pawn en passant.

There is no rule allowing a draw by repeating moves or checking the King. The rule concerns only the same position occurring three times. If you are seeking a draw and if a move is required in order to repeat the position a third time, do not make the move! It must be your turn to move to claim the draw. If you make the claim and make the move that repeats the position a third time without having a witness your opponent might falsely say you never made the claim before moving. To protect yourself and be able to prove that you claimed a draw when it was your turn to move you should write the move down in your score book, stop the clock, and summon a tournament director. Make the claim directly to the tournament director. If your opponent agrees the game immediately ends in a draw. If your opponent disagrees the tournament director will investigate by checking your score book.

Whoever claims a draw by repetition of position must have the moves written down in order to have the claim granted. The exception is when there are fewer than five minutes left during sudden death time control, the claim can be validated by a tournament director, deputy, or impartial witness. Also, with fewer than five minutes left during sudden death time control you may stop the clock to demonstrate to the tournament director the ability to force a draw by repetition of position without actually having to make the moves on the board. If a draw is claimed by repetition of position and the claim is found to be incorrect, two minutes will be added to the opponent's clock.

A *"draw by agreement"* can be made by the players. I have seen higher-rated players get a draw in a lost position simply by offering their opponent a draw. As a general rule, if you know you are winning you should not accept a draw by agreement even if your opponent is considerably higher rated. An exception might be if you were just slightly ahead in the game and all you needed was a draw in the last round of a tournament to win clear first place. Some years ago at a national championship one of my students told me after his game was over that his opponent (who was the official World Champion for his age category) offered a draw after losing a piece. When my student declined the offer his opponent then offered him a thousand dollars to accept the draw! My student declined the offer again and went on to defeat his opponent. It is highly illegal to prearrange the results of a game or bribe your opponent to give you a win or draw. Such an offer should be reported to the tournament director immediately, though proving it may be difficult without a witness.

The proper way to offer a draw is to first make your move, offer the draw, and then press the clock. Your opponent has until touching a piece to accept the draw. Your opponent may either accept or decline the draw verbally or decline the draw by making a move without saying anything. It is considered improper (and an annoyance) to offer a draw when it is your opponent's turn to move. Continuously offering a draw is also considered improper. In either case you should report it to the tournament director.

The *"fifty-move rule"* is designed to allow a game to finish within a reasonable period of time when one of the players doesn't know how to checkmate with a limited amount of material left on the board or if no progress can be made (i.e., the position is locked up and a breakthrough isn't going to occur). A draw using the fifty-move rule can be claimed by the player who has the turn to move by proving that at least fifty moves have been made without any Pawn being moved or piece captured. You will need to have the moves written down to prove this except when there are fewer than five minutes left during sudden death time control, when the tournament director or someone he assigns may count moves. You would need to stop your clock and ask the tournament director to do this. It will be necessary for the tournament director to agree that the position is simplified and that this rule may apply.

When there isn't enough material left on the board for it to be possible for a checkmate to occur the *"insufficient mating material"* rule ends the game in a draw. Here are the situations where this rule is applied:

1) When there are only two Kings left on the board,
2) When one player has only a King and the other side has only a King and a Bishop (or a King and a Knight),
3) When both players have only a King and Bishop left with the Bishops being on the same color squares.

ILLEGAL MOVES AND ILLEGAL POSITIONS

If during a game it is discovered that one of the player's last ten moves was illegal, the position shall be reinstated to what it was before the illegal move was made. The player who made the illegal move must observe all of the conditions of the touch-move rule after the position is reinstated (if the piece that was touched to make the illegal move can be moved to another square, it must be moved, or if an opponent's piece was touched when making an illegal move and it could be captured with another piece then that piece must be captured). Many players forget to enforce the touch-move rule after the position is corrected! You should also be sure that the tournament director doesn't forget to have two minutes added onto your clock after the position is corrected if your opponent made the illegal move.

Unless a player is in time trouble, having two minutes added to the clock is not much of an incentive to make a claim that an illegal move was made by an opponent. After an illegal move is made either player who discovers it could take up to nine moves (only one move when there are fewer than five minutes left during sudden death time control) after it was made to decide which position is better, the current one or the one just before the illegal move was made. At any point before the tenth move is reached, if a player wants to go back to the position before the illegal move was made it is simply necessary to make a claim of an illegal move! This is a major disadvantage if you are the player who made an illegal move and you don't realize it. On this type of claim the tournament director can use either one or both of the players' score books to verify and correct the illegal move.

If the opponent deliberately makes illegal moves the tournament director may invoke a penalty. However, the claim of a deliberate illegal move may be difficult if not impossible to prove.

If any of the pieces on the board were incorrectly set up at the beginning of the game and it is discovered before Black's tenth move the game is annulled and a new one started without any adjustment made on the clock. At any point of the game, if it is discovered that the game started with the board set up with a Black square in the lower right hand corner instead of a White square then the pieces will be transferred to a correctly placed board.

If during a game a piece is accidentally knocked over when a move is being made it is the responsibility of the player making the move to pick up the piece and place it on the correct square before the clock is punched. Knocking over pieces is not uncommon when a player is in serious time trouble. If your opponent knocks over a piece and presses the clock without correcting it, immediately press your clock to restart your opponent's time and tell your opponent to correct the problem on his own time! This will usually cause your opponent to lose a lot more time on his clock than if he had properly replaced the piece in the first place. This should also be reported to the tournament director.

SPECTATORS, INTERFERENCE, AND CONDUCT DURING GAMES

Spectators, or players in other games, are not to interfere in anyway with games in progress. If you are being bothered by a spectator who is standing too close to your game, making any disruptive movements, or making noises, then bring this to the attention of the tournament director. It is recommended that coaches, friends, or relatives stand behind the player they are watching to help reduce the chances of any claims that they may be assisting the player.

A player may not receive any assistance in his games, whether solicited or not. This applies to other players giving advice, the use of written material, additional chess sets, and computers. You should not talk to anyone during your game, unless with the permission of and in the presence of a tournament director. Otherwise you may immediately be suspected of receiving illegal advice.

It is illegal to distract or annoy your opponent in any manner whatsoever. If you feel that your opponent is doing anything to violate this important rule immediately report it to a tournament director. Some examples that I have seen that qualify as a violation of this rule include humming, singing, talking to one's self, talking to others, talking to an opponent (this is a big one!), making noises (that I cannot describe), tapping on the table, making constant movements with hands, legs, or head, bouncing up and down in a chair, making faces at the opponent, listening to loud music on a headset, and even nose-picking and flinging the ejecta at the opponent! One player even began to catch flying insects during the game. These imaginary insects were a great distraction to the opponent who sat there watching in amazement. Finally the tournament director took notice when the student stood up on the table and was jumping in the air to catch them. As mentioned, *immediately report such behavior*.

Psychology in Chess

In no other sport does psychology play as important a role as it does in chess. Chess is a pure mental sport. The implication of this is that a player's mental state has a great effect on performance. Therefore, improving performance means improving the condition of your mind.

Some of the various aspects of playing chess where psychology comes into play are visualization and perception of images, intuition, creativity, attention, calculation, self-confidence, and motivation. Entire chess books have been written on these subjects. We will focus on the more important and practical aspects of chess psychology for the scholastic tournament player. The most important aspects dealing with attention are related to fatigue, which I dealt with under Tournament Conditioning in Chapter One. I will discuss intuition and calculation under the section on analysis. I am not going to discuss creativity in this book. It is a very intangible subject that, in chess, has a lot to do with intuition and pattern recognition. One other problem I will deal with is that of playing the board instead of the opponent.

MOTIVATION

Winning a game of chess is in itself a major motivation for most scholastic players. Almost no one likes to lose. Most players find that chess is a great mental challenge as well as being a battlefield where opposing minds meet. These may seem to be enough reasons to play chess. However, it is a good idea to set some additional goals. Achieving each goal will then provide motivation for additional goals.

Setting realistic goals in chess is very important. Goals should be achievable based on your talent and what you plan to do to work toward your goals. It is a good idea to have numerous goals, keeping in mind that goals can be short term, intermediate, or long term. Setting up goals that indicate improvement in your playing ability is important for the tournament competitor. We will now discuss some possible goals for you to set.

Achieving a certain rating within a set time period is a good goal. Keep in mind that ratings are affected by how many rated games you play, the ratings of your opponents, and the results of each game. Therefore, *don't set a goal to achieve a rating too high if you cannot play in enough tournaments to make it possible!*

We will now take a look at one example of setting up a goal to reach a certain rating. Let's say you have an established rating of 1000 and want to set an intermediate goal of getting your rating up to 1200. You should have an idea of how long it will take you to play enough rated games to make your goal realistic. If you were playing in one tournament a month with an average of five rated games against players with an average rating the same as yours you would gain 16 points for each win. By doing the math you find you will need at least 13 wins to gain 200 points without any losses or draws. You cannot expect to win every game so you should account for this in your calculations. Therefore, it would be very difficult to achieve this goal in a three-month period based on only five rated games a month. Setting your goal of reaching a rating of 1200 within six months would be more realistic. Another option is that you may consider playing in more tournaments.

A long-term goal to become an Expert or Master by a certain age is not a bad idea. However, keep in mind that it usually takes many years of dedicated play, training, and a certain degree of talent to become such a strong player. Don't forget that just playing games alone will make it less likely that you would achieve your goal. Serious study and working with your chess teacher should be part of a well-rounded plan to improve. Remember that by setting unrealistic goals for either the short- or long-term you will only set yourself up for failure. This is true not only in chess but in everything.

Besides trying to improve your rating there are other goals you can set. Some examples, depending on where you are, can be to achieve a certain score or win a certain prize in a tournament. My students love to compete for trophies in local scholastic tournaments. However, some of my more advanced students set goals to win the state or national championships.

There are even college scholarships available for successful chess students who also do well in school. Keep in mind that it is important to get good school grades. Don't place your hopes on becoming a top-notch chess player or trainer at the expense of doing well in school. Some people have the idea that a typical national scholastic champion spends almost every waking hour on chess. This idea is totally false. Most of my national scholastic champions do well in school and are involved in at least one other sport. They achieve their success through efficient study, lessons, and play. The average national scholastic champion that I train takes one or two lessons a week, plays in a tournament every two or three weeks, studies chess several hours a week, and plays online and/or at his local chess club several times a week.

Some scholastic chess clubs give certificates for completing a course of study. This is a good psychological boost for many students. It gives them a sense of accomplishment. At the club that I run there are three levels of group classes that students can progress through. We also have a one-year pin for students who stay in the club for a year and an advanced-level cap that students can get only if they achieve a certain rating based on their age. Some clubs have a ladder system to enhance competition at their club.

SELF-CONFIDENCE

An important aspect of doing well in tournament competition is being self-confident. Doing what it takes to promote your own self-confidence and not enhancing your opponent's self-confidence will help you to win more games. This doesn't mean that you should act in a conceited manner or put others down. *Self-confidence is a belief in yourself and your abilities: Conceit is self-deception*. If you act arrogant and conceited you will soon not have any friends and it is important to have friends. Not only will you feel better about yourself if you treat others with kindness and respect but you will have other people to share ideas and enjoyment with. Some of my best national scholastic champions are also known to be nice kids.

When you play it is a good idea to sit using good posture. You should sit up straight and look confident like you are King. I have seen some players stand during games. Standing makes it difficult to relax and focus on your game, and it requires the use of more energy.

One of the worst habits some players have during games is to have their hands hover over the piece that they are thinking of moving. Showing hesitation before making a move shows a lack of confidence in what you are doing. This can only help boost your opponent's self-confidence. Also, placing your hand over the board without immediately moving blocks your view and you may be falsely accused of touching a piece. You also shouldn't point or use your hands in any way while you are analyzing.

Your hands have no brains in them and can get easily get you into trouble. I tell my students to "strike like a tiger!" Keep your hands away from the board until you have decided on your move. Once you are absolutely certain what your move is going to be, make it quickly and with confidence. *Always try to look like you know what you are doing*.

How long you should take on any given move depends on a variety of factors. The main factors are how much time you have on the clock and how complicated the position is. The last point relates directly to how far ahead you can reasonably calculate.

I once heard a story where a reporter asked the famous master Jose Capablanca, "How many moves do you see ahead?" He jokingly said, "Fifty!" The reporter, not knowing much about chess, wrote that down in his notes and then proceeded to ask another famous master, Richard Réti, the same question. Réti said "One! But always the right one." There is something to be learned from this. You need to see only as deep as necessary to establish the best move for the position.

Distributing the limited time given on the clock is a problem for some players. Some players are always getting themselves into serious time trouble due to poor time management. You must learn to pace yourself. Don't sit there and waste your time thinking when you have an obviously forced move (often a recapture or a lack of options to get out of check). You can always think on your opponent's time (when it is the opponent's turn to move). This is especially useful when you are short of time. However, if you have plenty of time on your clock and you think you see a good move, take the time for a second look, *there may be a better move*.

Sometimes when one player gets into time trouble and is forced to move quickly, the player with plenty of time on the clock also moves quickly in an attempt to run the opponent out of time. This often results in the player who isn't in time trouble blundering and losing! Unless your move is obvious, if you have the time to think, use it to make good moves. On the other hand, some players always try to be perfectionists. This is a good trait if you have a lot of thinking time. However, if you have a fast time control or are short of time on the clock you should look for a "good move" and not lose on time by always looking for the best move.

In the final round of a Swiss system tournament players close in ability are usually playing each other. At the end of a major scholastic tournament take a look at the games on the top boards in the highest section and the bottom boards in the lowest section. You will notice that the lower-rated players are moving much faster and that the games are finishing much quicker than the games on the top boards. Beginners tend to move too quickly. I tell my beginning players, *"If you do not think, your moves will stink!"*

The way a person is dressed or groomed also may have a psychological effect on an opponent. My students own a team uniform (cap, shirt, and jacket) and wear it when they attend chess events. As a coach it makes it easy for me to find my players quickly in a large crowd or at a distance. Moreover, wearing a team uniform and being identified as belonging to a club that is known for producing strong players can be beneficial.

At a team match I had one of the players from the opposing team walk up to me and ask if I could have my student take off the cap during their game. The student told me that every time he looked up he would see the cap and couldn't see the student's eyes. I informed him that everyone on my team always wears a cap. Of course, during a regular tournament coaches and players with games in progress should not talk to one another, unless in the presence of a tournament director. However, this was a team match and the coach on the other team didn't object. Some of my students also like the idea of keeping the overhead lights from directly hitting their eyes by wearing a cap.

At a national championship a player whom I had never before met walked up to me and boasted that he just played a student wearing a Chess for Juniors team uniform and got a draw. He was extremely happy about it. I asked this player for the name of the student he just played and then asked him what his rating was. I discovered that my student was rated several hundred points below him! This player was under the illusion that everyone wearing a Chess for Juniors uniform was a strong player. Many chess trainers who take their students to the nationals will also take weaker players so that they can gain experience. Most students wearing a team uniform have received some instruction. However, you will also find a lot of beginners wearing team uniforms.

Another aspect of building self-confidence is not to start a game (or tournament) with the idea that you are going to lose. Some players go into a game against a more experienced player resigned to the idea that they are going to lose. This can become what is known as the *self-fulfilling prophecy*. In this scenario, players will miss opportunities to win or draw against their more experienced opponent even when the opponent makes bad moves! Often players who expect to lose are so focused on how the opponent will win that they are blindsided and miss opportunities. Self-confidence is the solution for this type of attitude. Players should start a game with the attitude that no matter what the opponent's rating or reputation they will play their best, and if the opponent makes mistakes they will try to punish the mistakes. Remember that even a big dog worries about a little one that runs around nipping at his heels. After a game is over it is always a good idea to analyze it, regardless of the final outcome. Players can learn from mistakes made in games whether they are won, lost, or drawn.

PLAYING THE BOARD INSTEAD OF THE PERSON

Deliberately making a move that you know is inferior, in order to set up a trap that works only if your opponent makes a bad move, is rarely good strategy. The stronger your competition becomes the less likely it is that cheap traps will work. As a general rule *you should play the board instead of the person*. This means *don't make moves designed to set unsound traps or moves you feel would unsettle your opponent but are not good moves.* You should assume in most cases that your opponent sees what you see. Therefore, you should try to make the very best move while taking into consideration your opponent's best reply.

The exception to playing the board and not the person is when you are so far behind in material and hopelessly lost that you don't stand a chance unless a miracle happens. Well, in scholastic tournaments miracles happen! It is often said that good players are lucky. A good player will make the best out of what appears to be a hopeless situation. Let's say you were a Queen behind in an endgame. In this case your only hope (other than getting a stalemate) may be to threaten a back-rank checkmate that can be stopped in many ways. If you didn't have a checkmate threat you might make a Knight move that threatens to fork his King and Queen. Even though this type of play is inferior, if your opponent sees what you are up to, it may still be your only practical chance of saving yourself. Generally, going for a stalemate is the last resort in a hopeless situation.

Playing an opening that you know is weak because you think that your opponent may not know how to handle it is usually bad strategy. An example of this is the *"Scholar's Mate,"* also sometimes called the *"Four-Move Checkmate."* White brings the Queen out too early to create a simple checkmate threat that can be easily stopped and give Black a good game. A decent player will never become a victim of the Scholar's

Mate. Another reason I tell my students not to use the Scholar's Mate is because they will not be gaining experience in playing proper openings. We will now take a detailed look at how easily Black gets a good game against the Scholar's Mate by using a game played between two scholastic players.

1 e4 e5 2 Qh5

White initiates the Scholar's Mate by bringing his Queen out on the second move of the game! The Queen on "h5" threatens Black's undefended Pawn on "e5" and attacks Black's Pawn on "f7".

2...Nc6

This develops a minor piece while defending the Pawn on "e5". A common mistake made by beginners is to prematurely attempt to attack and drive away Black's Queen with 2...g6??. This allows 3 Qxe5+, forking Black's King and Rook.

3 Bc4

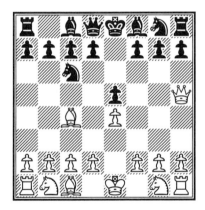

Diagram 4. Position after 3 Bc4

White develops a Bishop and attacks Black's Pawn on "f7" with a second piece. Only Black's King defends his Pawn on "f7". Therefore, White is threatening 4 Qxf7++.

3...g6

Black prevents checkmate by blocking Black's Queen. The Queen must now retreat since Black's Pawn is threatening her.

4 Qf3

White attacks Black's Pawn on "f7" and again threatens 5 Qxf7++.

4...Nf6

Black makes a constructive developing move while blocking Black's Queen from capturing on "f7". Black is now threatening to post his Knight actively and attack White's Queen and Pawn on "c2" with 5...Nd4.

5 Qb3?

White is getting carried away with the idea of threatening Black's Pawn on "f7". Therefore, White's Queen swings over to the "a2-g8" diagonal to threaten 6 Bxf7+.

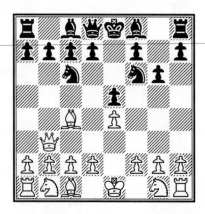

Diagram 5. Position after 5 Qb3.

It would have been better to develop a minor piece and cover the "d4" square with 5 Ne2. However, Black would still have a good game after 5...Na5.

See if you can find Black's winning move without looking at the next move in the game.

5...Nd4!

White's attack on "f7" is ignored! Black posts his Knight actively with an attack on White's exposed Queen and weak "c2" square. White must also concern himself about his undefended Pawn on "e4", since Black's Knight on "f6" is attacking it.

6 Bxf7+

White thinks he is doing well. The appearance of winning a Pawn and exposing Black's King to attack is only an illusion. We will soon see that it is White who is in trouble.

White could have played 6 Qd3 to get the Queen out of attack while defending the "c" and "e" Pawns. However, White would lose material after 6...d5! 7 Bxd5 (if 7 Bb3 then 7...Nxe4, or if 7 exd5 then 7...Bf5 with the idea of 8...Nxc2+ after White's Queen moves) Nxd5 8 exd5 Bf5 with the idea of 9...Nxc2+ after White's Queen moves.

6...Ke7

Now White must get his Queen out of attack while keeping his Bishop on "f7" and Pawn on "c2" protected.

7 Qc4

Black now has a move that wins White's Bishop in two moves. See if you can find Black's best move here without looking at the next move in the game.

7...b5

White's Queen is now driven away from the defense of the Bishop. After 8 Qd3 Black plays 8...Kxf7.

ANALYSIS AND EVALUATION

We use analysis to evaluate and reach a conclusion, based on our experience, as to what the best choice is in a given position. Two major components used during analysis are calculation and intuition. Through experience we develop pattern recognition. Pattern recognition is visualizing similar themes in the interaction of pieces on the board. Pattern recognition is the key element in our ability to calculate and use intuition.

Intuition at the chessboard is a subconscious ability that allows us to quickly understand a situation through the use of pattern recognition. An experienced player may quickly see the right move or plan in a position without consciously realizing how the conclusion was reached. This might sound contradictory, but many of the thought processes during play become so natural that the player doesn't realize that every step hasn't been consciously calculated.

You might compare this to the quick reflex actions that a professional tennis player uses while playing. A professional tennis player is trained to quickly respond to situations without having to consciously work out every movement, step by step. The experienced chess mind works in a similar way.

NEGATIVE IMAGES

An imperfection in the way an image is perceived on the board is often the reason why a mistake is made. To understand what causes error when analyzing will help you to correct your faults.

The most common image that causes players to make mistakes during analysis is the *"retained image."* This happens when you don't account for the change or changes for one or more pieces in a position after moves have been made. To state it another way, you keep the effects of one or more pieces from the past position that have now moved, been captured, or become pinned and project it into your current or future analysis. In this case the piece or pieces involved no longer have the same possibilities available even though you visualize and think these possibilities still exist. Sometimes players will refer to this as "seeing ghosts." This is because the player may have thought that a piece from the past was still there when analyzing. The best treatment for problems involving images is to study positions similar to those that give you difficulty and thereby improve your pattern recognition. We will now take a look at a few examples taken from actual play where a retained image resulted in a fatal mistake.

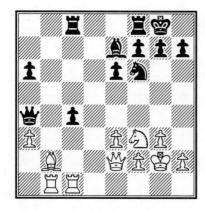

Diagram 6. White to move.

In Diagram 6 White played **1 Ne5??**, realizing that Black could sacrifice his "c" Pawn and clear the way for his Queen to go to "e4" with an attack on White's King and Rook on "b1". However, White noted that in the current position that his Rook on "b1" was protected by his Rook on "c1". After 1 Ne5 the game continued **1...c3! 2 Bxc3 Rxc3!** (taking advantage of White's Rook on "c1" being an overworked defender) **3 Rxc3 Qe4+**. White realized his Rook on "b1" was no longer defended since the Rook on "c1" has moved!

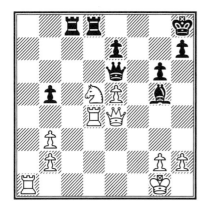

Diagram 7. Black to move.

Black has two Rooks covering his first rank preventing White's Rook from penetrating to "a8". Therefore, Black felt confident that he could aggressively attack White's Knight on "d5" with one of the Rooks and played **1...Rc5??**. White continued with **2 Nc7** (2 Nf4 would also work) and Black resigned because he realized that his plan to play 2...Rxd4 3 Nxe6 (3 Ra8+ would also win) Rxe4 allows a back-rank mate after 4 Ra8+ Rc8 5 Rxc8++.

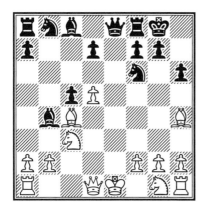

Diagram 8. White to move.

It is also possible to retain the partial effect of a piece from its previous location after it has moved from previous analysis. In Diagram 8 White analyzed that 1 Ne2 (blocking the check) would give Black a major advantage after 1...Bxc3+ 2 bxc3 Qe4. However, White noted that he would be able to prevent the immediate loss of a piece with 3 Bxf6 Qxc4 4 Be7 Re8 5 d6 Ba6. White rejected this line because he ends up with a horrible position. White actually played **1 Kf1??** and the game continued **1...Bxc3 2 bxc3 Qe4**. White at this point realized that he would now lose a piece after 3 Bxf6 because 3...Qxc4 is now placing White's King on "f1" in check!

An *"inert image"* occurs when a player feels that a position is reached during analysis where his goal is achieved and no great thought is required from that point onward. The player becomes confident in his analysis and blindly proceeds toward that position. Here is where intuition can fail! Let us take a look at an example of this.

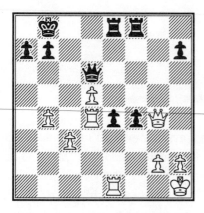

Diagram 9. Black to move.

Black saw an idea that involves sacrificing his "h" Pawn to open the "h" file for his Rook and advancing his "f" Pawn to open the "h2-b8" diagonal for his Queen. At the end of the variation all that Black saw is that White's Queen is lost because if she moves off the h-file Black would play Qxh2++. So Black proceeded to play **1...h5 2 Qxh5 f3**. Because of the threat 3...Rh8 Black never considered that White would capture on "f3" (note this also involves a retained image). When White played **3 gxf3!** Black should have stopped to think again. If he did he would have realized that he should play 3...Re5. However, he blindly continued with what he had analyzed from the beginning as a winning position and played **3...Rh8??**. He overlooked **4 Rdxe4!**. The game quickly ended after **4...Rxh5 5 Rxe8+ Kc7 6 R1e7+ Kb6 7 Re6**.

A *"forward image"* is where possible future threats are so overestimated that they seem to exist in the present. In reality the perceived threats may never materialize. However, because the threats seem real this often causes a player to overreact and play inaccurately.

A common example of the forward image among some beginners is their extreme fear of losing to a back-rank mate after they have castled. Some beginners have told me that they will never castle or that they will always move a Pawn near the King immediately after castling to avoid any possibility of a back-rank mate. This kind of over-reaction to potential threats that don't exist will cause serious mistakes to be made. It is important to realize that there is a big difference between a real threat and a potential threat. *It is good to be aware of potential threats, but not to overreact to them.*

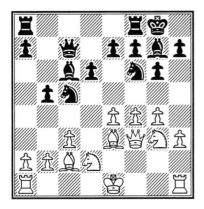

Diagram 10. White to move.

The position in Diagram 10 provides us with a classic example of a forward image causing an overreaction to a Kingside attack. White continued his massive Pawn build-up on the Kingside with **1 h4**. If Black does nothing White will continue his Pawn storm and Black will meet certain death. The correct plan for Black would have been to seek counter-play on the Queenside with a move such as 1...b4, planning to meet 2 cxb4 with 2...Na6 3 a3 Bd7. However, Black has so much fear of White's mass of Pawns on the Kingside that he tried to directly attack them with **1...e5?**. This allowed White to continue with **2 f5** threatening 3 g5. Black didn't survive the attack.

Preparing an Opening System— Setting Up Opening Charts

Before the middlegame and endgame comes the opening. If you do not survive the opening the knowledge that you have about the other parts of the game will not be of any use. It is difficult to overstate the importance of being well prepared in the opening.

The key to being well prepared in the opening is the construction and study of a well thought out opening system. Selecting openings and individual lines for your personal system takes time and isn't an easy task. Therefore, to make this task easier, you should keep in mind these common factors found in a good opening system:

1) *The lines in your system should be sound.* Although this may sound like an obvious point, it is often neglected. Sometimes players will prepare an opening that they know is weak because they may like a trap or an attack even though it isn't sound. Sometimes players are attracted by the exotic nature of certain openings. We have already seen that the concept of playing something weak with the hope that the opponent doesn't know the refutation is bad strategy. If it is known

that you play an inferior opening line your opponents can look it up and are then prepared with the refutation. You would likely be forced to discard the inferior opening, thereby wasting the time you spent preparing it. It is just as easy to do research on an opening that is sound and avoid a waste of time.

2) *The lines in your system should take into consideration what is in common use.* Some openings or individual variations go through fashions just like music and clothing. Sometimes a top player will use a certain opening line and, like sheep, a lot of players will start to use it. Just because an opening line is fashionable doesn't mean it is strong! In fact, many less popular openings are very strong, and your opponents are less likely to be prepared against them.

Even though you may want to spend more time focusing on the most popular openings in your opening system, it is important for you to also prepare for the less popular lines. For example, more effort should go into preparing as Black against 1 e4 or 1 d4 than against less popular and weaker openings like 1 b4 or 1 g4.

3) *The lower-rated player should develop a well-rounded system that is instructive.* The developing player's system should consist of openings that give exposure to a variety of tactical situations and concepts. This will help you develop a style with which you feel comfortable. Lower-rated players have more difficulty grasping deep positional concepts. It takes more experience to develop an understanding of positional play. This point needs to be considered when deciding which openings and lines are to be included in your system. I personally like to teach my beginning-level players to open games with 1 e4 e5.

4) *The intermediate or advanced player needs to consider individual style in his opening system.* Whereas lower-rated players are just beginning to develop a style, more advanced players should have some idea of what their style of play is. It is important that you feel comfortable with the openings you play and take your personal style into consideration when selecting the openings in your system.

PREPARATION AND STUDY

Books and computer databases provide you with your most detailed source of information. They provide you with opening lines and in many cases evaluations along with the ideas behind the moves. Thousands of chess books have been written about the opening.

For beginning or intermediate players I recommend *Ideas Behind the Chess Openings* by Reuben Fine (New York: Random House, 1990). Its coverage has a good balance between opening lines and the ideas behind these lines. For intermediate or advanced players, I recommend *Modern Chess Openings* by Nick deFirmian (New York: Random House, 1999). This book contains extensive coverage of all major openings and it provides evaluation of the lines it covers.

Some sources tell students never to memorize opening lines. This is totally incorrect! When studying the opening it is important to both understand the ideas behind the moves and to know the main lines of your system. Having the main lines of your opening system memorized will save you an enormous amount of time on your clock. This is time that can better be used in the middlegame or endgame.

You should go over each move carefully to understand the reason behind the moves. If your opponent deviates from the book line, then you can compare the ideas behind the book move to the move that was played. That will give you clues about how to proceed.

Often players will get a bad position out of the opening and want to immediately discard their opening line. Instead of discarding part of a system that you have invested a lot of time in, it is best to carefully review the line in question. See where you went wrong and try to find an improvement for the next time you play this opening. Sometimes a player will discover a mistake or weakness in his opening system. However, *don't quickly discard an opening line from future use unless you are certain it is unsound*. Give your opening system a chance! For the more advanced player, keep in mind that opening theory is constantly changing and improving. *Be open to change*!

For all practical purposes the number of opening lines that exist may be compared to the number of grains of sand on the beach or number of stars in the universe. Good players limit the number of lines that they prepare. *Specialization is the key to success*! Because there is so much material to study you should prepare your own personal opening charts in an outline form. Using a word processor on a computer is much better than trying to write down every line by hand. You will find that you will be constantly making changes to update and improve your system. Being able to print out your system and take it everywhere with you is a major convenience. You can quickly refer to it at tournaments to prepare for opponents you know are likely to play certain openings. Remember that *it is illegal to use your opening charts while your tournament game is in progress*.

Unless you are already an experienced tournament player with a large opening repertoire you should begin charting your system by preparing only one possible move against each of your opponents' most likely moves. For example, against 1 e4 you would prepare the response 1...e5. You would stick strictly to meeting 1 e4 with 1...e5 as Black, disregarding any other response. The same treatment is given for each and every move written down in your system. This will allow you to greatly limit the amount of material you need to study. You will cut out a number of opening lines that would never be reached in your system. This saves a lot of work and helps you focus on what is most important.

A beginning or intermediate level scholastic player who meets 1 e4 with 1...e5 on Monday, 1...c5 on Tuesday, 1...c6 on Wednesday, 1...e6 on Thursday and 1...Nf6 on Friday is certainly a jack-of-all-trades but master of none. Most players will have little chance of gaining a deep understanding of any one of these openings if they try to learn them all and use them at the same time.

When a player becomes more advanced and knows his opening system well, it may become necessary to expand by adding more than one possible response to moves in the system. My most advanced players are watched carefully, and their opponents prepare against them. Therefore, it is necessary for them to expand on their opening system. Just how detailed your system should be depends on how much time you have, the availability of material covering your system, and what you feel will make you comfortable in the opening. If you feel you have improvements or additional analysis that isn't in a book or database, then you should feel free to include that in your charts. Keep in mind that books and databases aren't perfect and sometimes contain errors.

You will find on the following pages a very comprehensive example of an opening chart that is similar to what some of my students use. The system found here is well-rounded for all levels of players. You will find either that these recommended lines will be a good starting place for you or that they will help you build on what you already play.

The charts are set up in a typical outline form with the most important lines underlined and in bold face. At the next level of importance are the lines that are only boldfaced. Keep in mind that this chart does not cover every possible opening line that can be played against someone using this system. The ideas behind the moves and evaluations are not given. In this way the charts are kept in a very condensed form and are easy to use. Those wanting to know the ideas behind many of these lines should consult my book *Unbeatable Chess Lessons for Juniors* (New York: Random House, 2003).

Be sure not to confuse lines you are to play as White with lines as Black. In the first section the charts are set up for play as White.

OPENING SYSTEM AS WHITE

RUY LOPEZ

1 e4 e5 2 Nf3 Nc6 3 Bb5 a6 4 Ba4 Nf6 5 0-0 now,

- A) 5...Nxe4 6 d4 b5 (6...exd4? 7 Re1 d5 8 Nxd4) 7 Bb3 d5 8 dxe5 Be6 9 c3 Bc5 10 Nbd2 0-0 11 Bc2.
- B) 5...Be7 6 Re1 b5 7 Bb3 now,
  1) 7...0-0 8 c3 d5 9 exd5 Nxd5 (9...e4 10 dxc6 exf3 11 d4 fxg2 12 Qf3) 10 Nxe5 Nxe5 11 Rxe5 c6 (11...Nf6 12 d4 Bd6 13 Re1 Ng4 14 h3 Qh4 15 Qf3 Nxf2 16 Bd2 Bb7 17 Qxb7 Nd3 18 Re2 Qg3 19 Kf1) 12 d4 Bd6 13 Re1 Qh4 14 g3 Qh3 15 Be3 Bg4 16 Qd3 Rae8 17 Nd2 Re6 18 a4 bxa4 19 Rxa4 f5 20 Qf1 Qh5 21 f4.
  2) 7...d6 8 c3 0-0 9 h3 Na5 10 Bc2 c5 11 d4 Qc7 (11...Nd7 12 dxc5 dxc5 13 Nbd2 f6 14 Nh4) 12 Nbd2 Bd7 13 Nf1 Rfe8 14 b3 cxd4 15 cxd4 Rac8 16 Ne3 g6 17 Bb2 Bf8 18 Rc1 Qb8.

1 e4 e5 2 Nf3 Nc6 3 Bb5 now,

- A) 3...f5 4 d3 fxe4 5 dxe4 Nf6 6 0-0 Bc5 (6...d6 7 Qd3) 7 Qe2 d6 8 Qc4 Qe7 9 Nc3 Bd7 10 Nd5 Nxd5 11 exd5 Nd4 12 Bxd7+ Qxd7 13 Nxe5 Qf5 14 Nd3 b5 15 Re1+ Kf7 16 Qc3 Qxd5 17 Be3 Qc4 18 Qxc4 bxc4 19 Nxc5 Nxc2 (19...dxc5 20 Rac1) 20 Na6 Rhc8 21 b4.
- B) 3...d6 4 d4 Bd7 5 Nc3 exd4 6 Nxd4 g6 7 0-0.
- C) 3...Nf6 4 0-0 Nxe4 (4...Bc5 5 c3) 5 d4 Nd6 (5...Be7 6 Qe2 Nd6 7 Bxc6 bxc6 8 dxe5) 6 Bxc6 dxc6 7 dxe5.
- D) 3...Bc5 4 c3 Nf6 (4...f5 5 d4 fxe4 6 Bxc6 dxc6 7 Nfd2) 5 0-0 0-0 6 d4.
- E) 3...Nd4 4 Nxd4 exd4 5 0-0 Bc5 6 d3 c6 7 Ba4 Ne7 8 f4 d5 (8...f5 9 Bb3 d5 10 exd5 Nxd5 11 Re1+) 9 f5 dxe5 (9...0-0 10 f6 gxf6 11 Qh5) 10 dxe4 0-0 11 Bb3.

PETROV'S DEFENSE

1 e4 e5 2 Nf3 Nf6 3 d4 now,

- A) 3...exd4 4 e5 Ne4 5 Qxd4 d5 6 exd6 Nxd6 7 Nc3 Nc6 8 Qf4 g6 9 Bd3 Bg7 10 Be3 Be6 11 0-0-0 Qf6 12 Qa4 Qe7 (12...h6 13 Bb5 Bd7 14 Bd4 Qf4+ 15 Rd2 0-0 16 Nd5) 13 Ne4 0-0 14 Rhe1 Nxe4 15 Bxe4 Rfd8 16 Rxd8+ Nxd8 17 Bd4.

B) <u>3...Nxe4 4 Bd3 d5 5 Nxe5 Nd7</u> (5...Bd6 6 0-0 0-0 7 Nd2 Bxe5 8 dxe5 Nc5 9 Nb3 Nxd3 10 Qxd3 Nc6 and now either 11 Qg3 or 11 Bf4 Qh4 12 Bg3 Qc4 13 Rad1 Nb4 14 Qxc4 dxc4 15 Nd4 c5 16 Nb5 Nxc2 17 Nc7 Rb8 18 e6 fxe6 19 Bd6) **6 Nxd7 Bxd7 7 0-0 Qh4** (7...Bd6 8 c4 c6 9 cxd5 cxd5 10 Qh5) **8 c4 0-0-0 9 c5 g5 10 Be3 Re8 11 Nd2 Bg7 12 Nf3**.

PHILIDOR'S DEFENSE

<u>1 e4 e5 2 Nf3 d6 3 d4 Nf6 4 Nc3 Nbd7 5 Bc4 Be7 6 0-0 0-0 7 Qe2 c6 8 Rd1 Qc7 9 a4</u>.

LATVIAN GAMBIT

<u>1 e4 e5 2 Nf3 f5 3 Nxe5 Qf6 4 d4 d6 5 Nc4 fxe4 6 Nc3 Qg6 7 Bf4 Nf6 8 Ne3 Be7 9 Qd2 c6 10 d5</u>.

QUEEN PAWN COUNTER GAMBIT

<u>1 e4 e5 2 Nf3 d5 3 exd5 e4</u> (3...Qxd5 4 Nc3 Qe6 5 Bb5+ c6 6 Ba4 Qg6 7 Qe2) **4 Qe2 Qe7** (4...Nf6 5 d3 Be7 6 dxe4 0-0 7 Bf4 Re8 8 Nbd2) **5 Nd4 Nf6 6 Nc3**.

SICILIAN DEFENSE

<u>1 e4 c5 2 f4</u> now,
- A) <u>2...d5 3 Nc3 e6</u> (3...dxe4 4 Nxe4 e6 5 Nf3 Nc6 6 Bb5 Bd7 7 0-0 Be7 8 d3 Nf6 9 c3 0-0 10 Nxf6+ Bxf6 11 Be3 Qb6 12 Bc4 Rfd8 13 Qe2) **4 Bb5+ Bd7 5 Bxd7+ Qxd7 6 d3 Nc6 7 Nf3 Nf6 8 0-0**.
- B) <u>2...e6 3 Nf3 d5 4 Bb5+ Bd7 5 Bxd7+ Qxd7</u> (5...Nxd7 6 d3) **6 Ne5 Qc7 7 exd5 exd5 8 Nc3 Nf6 9 Qf3 d4** (9...Qd8 10 Qe2) **10 Nb5 Qb6 11 Qb3**.
- C) <u>2...Nc6 3 Nf3</u> now,
  1) <u>3...d6 4 Bb5 Bd7 5 Nc3 g6 6 0-0 Bg7 7 d3</u>.
  2) <u>3...g6 4 Bb5 Bg7 5 Bxc6 bxc6 6 Nc3 d6 7 0-0 Rb8 8 d3 Nf6 9 Qe1 0-0 10 b3 Bg4 11 Bb2</u>.
  3) <u>3...e6 4 Nc3 d5 5 Bb5 Ne7 6 exd5 exd5</u> (6...Nxd5 7 Bxc6+ bxc6 8 d3) **7 Qe2**.
- D) <u>2...g6 3 Nf3 Bg7 4 Nc3 Nc6 5 Bb5 Nd4 6 a4 e6 7 d3 Ne7 8 e5 a6 9 Bc4 d5 10 exd6 Qxd6 11 Ne4 Qc7 12 c3 Ndf5 13 a5</u>.

FRENCH DEFENSE

<u>1 e4 e6 2 d4 d5 3 Nc3</u> now,

- A) <u>3...Bb4 5 e5 c5 5 Bd2</u> now,
  1) <u>5...cxd4 6 Nb5 Bxd2+ 7 Qxd2 Nc6 8 f4 Nge7 9 Nd6+ Kf8 10 Nf3 Qb6 11 0-0-0.</u>
  2) 5...Nc6 6 Nb5 Bxd2+ 7 Qxd2 Nxd4 8 Nxd4 cxd4 9 f4 Ne7 10 Nf3 Nc6 11 Nxd4 Qb6 12 0-0-0.
- B) <u>3...Nf6 4 Bg5</u> now,
  1) <u>4...Be7 5 e5 Nfd7 6 Bxe7 Qxe7 7 f4 0-0</u> (7...c5 8 Nb5) <u>8 Nf3 c5 9 dxc5 Nc6</u> ~~(9...Qxc5 10 Qd4 Nc6 11 Qxc5 Nxc5 12 a3 f6 13 exf6 Rxf6 14 g3)~~ <u>10 Bd3 f5 11 exf6 Qxf6 12 g3 Nxc5 13 0-0.</u>
  2) <u>4...Bb4 5 e5 h6 6 Bd2 Bxc3 7 bxc3 Ne4 8 Qg4 g6 9 Qf4 c5 10 Bd3 Nxd2 11 Qxd2 Nc6 12 Nf3 Qa5 13 dxc5 Qxc5 14 0-0 Bd7 15 Rab1.</u>
- C) 3...dxe4 4 Nxe4 Nd7 5 Nf3 Ngf6 6 Nxf6+ Nxf6 7 Bd3 c5 8 dxc5 Bxc5 9 Qe2 0-0 10 0-0 Qc7 11 Bg5.

CARO KANN DEFENSE

<u>1 e4 c6 2 d4 d5 3 Nc3 dxe4 4 Nxe4</u> now,

- A) <u>4...Nd7 5 Bc4 Ngf6 6 Ng5 e6 7 Qe2 Nb6 8 Bd3 h6</u> (8...Qxd4 9 N1f3 followed by 10 Ne5) <u>9 N5f3 c5 10 dxc5 Bxc5 11 Ne5 Nbd7 12 Ngf3 Qc7 13 0-0 0-0 14 Re1.</u>
- B) <u>4...Bf5 5 Ng3 Bg6 6 h4 h6 7 Nf3 Nd7 8 h5 Bh7 9 Bd3 Bxd3 10 Qxd3 Qc7 11 Bd2 e6 12 0-0-0 Ngf6 13 Ne4 0-0-0 14 g3.</u>
- C) <u>4...Nf6 5 Nxf6+ gxf6</u> (5...exf6 6 Bc4 Bd6 7 Qe2+ Qe7 8 Qxe7+ Kxe7 9 Ne2) <u>6 c3 Bf5 7 Ne2 Nd7 8 Ng3 Bg6 9 h4 h5 10 Be2 Qa5 11 b4 Qd5 12 0-0.</u>

ALEKHINE'S DEFENSE

<u>1 e4 Nf6 2 e5 Nd5 3 d4 d6 4 Bc4 Nb6</u> (4...e6 5 Nf3 Be7 6 0-0 0-0 7 Qe2, or if 4...c6 5 Qe2 dxe5 6 dxe5 g6 7 h3 Bg7 8 Nf3 0-0 9 0-0) <u>5 Bb3</u> now,

- A) 5...e6 6 Nf3 Nc6 7 Qe2 Be7 8 0-0 0-0 9 c3 dxe5 10 dxe5.
- B) 5...Nc6 6 e6 fxe6 7 Nf3 g6 (7...d5 8 Bf4 Nd7 9 c3 Nf6 10 h4) <u>8 Ng5 d5 9 Qf3 Nxd4 10 Qf7+ Kd7 11 c3.</u>
- C) 5...dxe5 6 Qh5 e6 7 dxe5 a5 (7...Nc6 8 Nf3 Nd4 9 Nc3) <u>8 a4 Na6 9 Nf3 Nc5 10 0-0 Nxb3 11 cxb3 Bd7 12 Nc3 Be7 13 Rd1.</u>

PIRC DEFENSE

1 e4 d6 2 d4 Nf6 3 Nc3 g6 4 g3 Bg7 5 Bg2 0-0 6 Nge2 now,

A) 6...Nbd7 7 0-0 c5 8 dxc5 Nxc5 9 Nf4 Bg4 10 Qe1 Bd7 11 Qe2 Bc6 12 Rd1.

B) 6...c6 7 0-0 e5 8 h3 Nbd7 9 Be3 Re8 10 f4.

C) 6...e5 7 0-0 Nc6 8 dxe5 dxe5 (8...Nxe5 9 f4 Ned7 10 h3 Re8 11 Be3) **9 Bg5 Nd4 10 Nxd4 exd4 11 Nd5 Be6 12 Qf3 Bxd5 13 exd5 Qd6 14 Rad1**.

CENTER COUNTER DEFENSE

1 e4 d5 2 exd5 now,

A) 2...Nf6 3 d4 Nxd5 (3...Bg4 4 f3 Bf5 5 Bb5+ Nbd7 6 c4 e6 7 dxe6 Bxe6 8 d5 Bf5 9 Nc3 Bc5 10 Qe2+ Qe7 11 Qxe7+ Bxe7 12 Nge2) **4 Nf3 Bg4** (4...g6 5 Be2 Bg7 6 0-0 0-0 7 c4 Nb6 8 Nc3 Nc6 9 d5 Ne5 10 Qb3) **5 Be2 Nc6 6 0-0 e6 7 c4 Nb6 8 Nc3 Bxf3 9 Bxf3 Nxc4 10 Re1 Be7 11 d5**.

B) 2...Qxd5 3 Nc3 Qa5 4 d4 Nf6 5 Nf3 Bf5 (5...Bg4 6 h3 Bh5 7 g4 Bg6 8 Ne5 e6 9 Bg2, 5...c6 transposes after 6 Bc4 Bf5 7 Bd2) **6 Bc4 c6 7 Bd2 e6 8 Qe2 now not 8...Bxc2? because of 9 d5!**.

OPENING SYSTEM AS BLACK

RUY LOPEZ

1 e4 e5 2 Nf3 Nc6 3 Bb5 a6 4 Bxc6 dxc6 5 0-0 (5 Nxe5 Qd4) **Qd6** now,

A) 6 c3 (6 Na3 b5) **Bg4 7 d4** (7 h3 Bxf3 10 Qxf3 0-0-0) **0-0-0 8 Be3 f5**.

B) 6 d3 Ne7 7 Be3 (7 Nbd2 Ng6 8 Nc4 Qf6 9 d4 exd4 10 Bg5 Qe6 11 Qxd4 f6 12 Rad1 Be7 13 Be3 0-0) **Ng6 8 Nbd2 Be7 9 d4 exd4 10 Nxd4 Ne5 11 h3 c5 12 Nb3 b6 13 f4 Nc6**.

C) 6 d4 exd4 now,

1) 7 Qxd4 Bg4 8 Qe3 (8 Nc3 Bxf3 9 Qxd6 Bxd6 10 gxf3 Ne7 11 f4 f6 12 Be3 0-0-0) **Ne7 9 Nbd2 Ng6 10 h3 Bd7 11 Nc4 Qc5**.

2) **7 Nxd4 Bd7 8 Nc3** (8 Be3 0-0-0 9 Nd2 Nh6 10 f3 f5 11 Qe2 Re8 12 Rfe1 Qg6 13 Bxh6 Qxh6 14 e5 c5) **0-0-0 9 Be3 Qg6 10 Qe2 Nh6 11 Rad1 Bd6 12 f3 Rhe8 13 Bf2 Qh5 14 Bg3 Bxg3 15 hxg3 f5**.

1 e4 e5 2 Nf3 Nc6 3 Bb5 a6 4 Ba4 Nf6 now,

- A) 5 Bxc6 dxc6 6 d3 Bd6 7 Nbd2 Be6 8 Qe2 Nd7 Nc4 f6 10 d4 Bg4.
- B) 5 d4 exd4 6 0-0 Be7 now,
  1) 7 e5 Ne4 8 Nxd4 (8 Re1 Nc5 9 Bxc6 dxc6 10 Nxd4 0-0 11 Nc3 f5 12 Nce2 Ne6) Nxd4 9 Qxd4 Nc5 10 Nc3 0-0 11 Be3 d6.
  2) 7 Re1 0-0 8 e5 Ne8 9 c3 (9 Nxd4 Nxd4 10 Qxd4 d5 11 exd6 Bxd6 12 c3 Bf5, or if 9 Bf4 b5 10 Bb3 d5) d3 10 Qxd3 d6 11 Bc2 g6 12 exd6 Nxd6 13 Bh6 Re8 14 Na3 Nf5.

1 e4 e5 2 Nf3 Nc6 3 Bb5 a6 4 Ba4 Nf6 5 0-0 Be7 now,

- A) 6 Bxc6 dxc6 7 d3 (7 Nc3 Nd7 8 d4 f6 9 Be3 0-0 10 Qe2 Qe8 11 Rfd1 Qh5 12 Ne1 Qxe2 13 Nxe2 Bd6, or if 7 Qe1 Nd7 8 d4 exd4 9 Nxd4 Nc5 10 Qe3 0-0 11 Nc3 Re8 12 Rd1 Bd6) Nd7 8 Nbd2 (8 d4 exd4 9 Nxd4 0-0 10 Nc3 Nb6 followed by c5) 0-0 9 Nc4 f6 10 d4 (10 Ne3 Nc5 11 Nf5 Bxf5 12 exf5 Qd5, or if 10 Nh4 Rf7 11 Nf5 Bf8) exd4 11 Nxd4 Nc5 12 f3 Re8 13 Be3 Bf8 14 Re1 Qe7 15 b3 Qf7 16 Qd2 Ne6.
- B) 6 Qe2 b5 7 Bb3 0-0 8 c3 d5 9 d3 (9 exd5 Bg4 10 dxc6 e4 11 d4 exf3 12 gxf3 Bh3 13 Re1 Re8 14 Bg5 Nd5) Re8 10 Nbd2 (10 exd5 Nxd5 11 Nxe5 Nxe5 12 Qxe5 Bb7 followed by Nf6, or if 10 Re1 Bb7 11 Nbd2 Bf8 12 Nf1 Na5 13 Bc2 c5) Bf8 11 Rd1 Na5 12 Bc2 c5 13 Nf1 d4 14 cxd4 exd4 15 Ng3 Qb6 16 Bd2 Bb7 17 Rac1 Rad8.

1 e4 e5 2 Nf3 Nc6 3 Bb5 a6 4 Ba4 Nf6 5 0-0 Be7 6 Re1 b5 7 Bb3 d6 8 c3 0-0 9 h3 (9 d4 Bg4 10 d5 Na5 11 Bc2 c6 12 dxc6 Qc7, or if 10 Be3 exd4 11 cxd4 d5 12 e5 Ne4 13 Nc3 Nxc3 14 bxc3 Qd7 15 h3 Bh5 16 Bf4 Na5 17 Bc2 Nc4, or if 10 h3 Bxf3 11 gxf3 Na5 12 Bc2 Nh5 13 f4 Nxf4 14 Bxf4 exf4 15 Qg4 Qc8 16 Qf3 c5) Na5 10 Bc2 c5 11 d4 Nd7 now,

- A) 12 d5 Nb6 13 g4 h5 14 Nh2 hxg4 15 hxg4 Bg5 16 Nd2 g6.
- B) 12 Bd3 exd4 13 cxd4 Nc6 14 Bf1 Bf6.
- C) 12 a4 Bb7 13Nbd2 Re8 14 NF1 exd4 15 Cxd4 Bf6 16 axb5 axb5 17 Qd3 C4.
- D) 12 b3 exd4 13 cxd4 Nc6 14 Nc3 Bf6 15 Be3 cxd4 16 Nxd4 Nxd4 17 Bxd4 Bb7 18 Bxf6 (18 Ne2 Re8 19 Ng3 g6) Qxf6 19 Re3 Rac8 20 Rd3 Rfd8.
- E) 12 dxc5 dxc5 13 Nbd2 Bb7 14 Nf1 Nc4.
- F) 12 Nbd2 cxd4 13 cxd4 Nc6 now,
  1) 14 d5 Nb4 15 Bb1 a5 16 Nf1 (16 a3 Na6 17 b4 Nb6 18 Qb3 Bd7 19 Bd3 Nc7 20 Rb1 Kh8 21 Bb2 f5 or 16 Qe2 Rb8 17 a3 Na6 18 Bd3 Nac5 19 b4 Nxd3 20 Qxd3 a4 21 Nf1 f5 22 exf5 Nb6 23 Qxb5 Bd7 24 Qe2 Nxd5 25 Qc4 Rb5 26 Ne3 Qc8) Rb8 17 g4 Na6 18 Ng3 g6 19 Kh2 Nac5.

2) **14 Nb3 a5 15 Bd3** (15 Be3 a4 16 Nbd2 Bf6 17 d5 Nb4 18 Bb1 Nc5 19 Nf1 Nba6, or if 16 Nc1 Bb7 17 Bd3 exd4 18 Nxd4 Nxd4 19 Bxd4 Bf6 20 Ne2 Re8) **Ba6 16 d5** (16 Be3 a4 17 Nc1 exd4 18 Nxd4 Nxd4 19 Bxd4 Ne5 20 Bf1Nc6 21 Be3 Bf6 22 Nd3 Bb7) **Nb4 17 Bf1 a4 18 Nbd4 exd4 19 a3 Nxd5 20 exd5 d3 21 Bxd3 Bf6 22 Rb1 Nc5 23 Bc2 Bb7 24 Nd4 Re8 25 Rxe8+ Qxe8.**

3) **14 Nf1 exd4 15 Nxd4 Nxd4 16 Qxd4 Ne5 17 Qd1** (17 Rd1 Bb7 18 Ng3 Bf6 19 Qxd6 Qc8 20 Qd2 Rd8 21 Qe2 Qc4 22 Rxd8+ Rxd8, or if 17 f4 Nc6 18 Qf2 Bh4 19 g3 Bf6 20 Rd1 Qc7 21 Kh2 Bb7 22 Bb1 Rfe8) **Bf6 18 Ne3 Be6 19 Nd5 Bxd5 20 exd5** (20 Qxd5 Rc8 21 Bb3 Nc4 22 Re2 Rc5 23 Qd1 d5) **Nc4 21 a4 Qa5 22 Ra2 Rfe8 23 Rf1 Rac8 24 Bb1 b4.**

GIUOCO PIANO

1 e4 e5 2 Nf3 Nc6 3 Bc4 Bc5 4 c3 Nf6 5 d4 (5 0-0 Nxe4 6 d4 exd4 7 cxd4 d5) **exd4 6 cxd4** (6 e5 d5 7 Bb5 Ne4 8 cxd4 Be7 9 Nc3 0-0 10 Bd3 f5) **Bb4+** now,

A) **7 Bd2 Bxd2+ 8 Nbxd2 d5 9 exd5 Nxd5 10 Qb3 Nce7 11 0-0 0-0 12 Re1 c6 13 a4 Qb6 14 a5 Qxb3 15 Nxb3 Rd8.**

B) **7 Nc3 Nxe4 8 0-0 Bxc3 9 d5** (9 bxc3 d5) **Bf6 10 Re1 Ne7 11 Rxe4 d6 12 Bg5** (12 g4 0-0 13 g5 Be5 14 Nxe5 dxe5 15 Rxe5 Ng6 16 Re1 Qd7) **Bxg5 13 Nxg5 h6 14 Qe2** (14 Bb5+ Bd7 15 Qe2 Bxb5 16 Qxb5+ Qd7 17 Qe2 Kf8) **hxg5 15 Re1 Be6 16 dxe6 f6 17 Re3 c6 18 Rh3 Rxh3 19 gxh3 g6 20 Qd2 Kf8 21 h4 gxh4 22 Qh6+ Kg8 23 Re3 Qa5 24 Qxh4 Kg7 25 Rh3 Qg5+ 26 Qxg5 fxg5.**

EVANS GAMBIT

1 e4 e5 2 Nf3 Nc6 3 Bc4 Bc5 4 b4 Bxb4 5 c3 Ba5 6 d4 d6 7 Qb3 (7 0-0 Bb6) **Qd7 8 dxe5 Bb6 9 exd6 Na5 10 Qb4 Nxc4 11 Qxc4 Qxd6 11 Ba3 Be6.**

PONZIANI OPENING/SCOTCH GAME/GORING GAMBIT

1 e4 e5 2 Nf3 Nc6 3 d4 (3 c3 d5 4 Qa4 f6 5 Bb5 Ne7 6 exd5 Qxd5, or if 4 Bb5 dxe4 5 Nxe5 Qd5) **exd4** now,

A) **4 Nxd4 Nf6 5 Nc3** (5 Nxc6 bxc6 6 e5 Qe7 7 Qe2 Nd5 8 c4 Ba6 9 b3 Qh4 10 a3 Bc5) **Bb4 6 Nxc6 bxc6 7 Bd3 d5 8 exd5 cxd5 9 0-0 0-0 10 Bg5 c6 11 Qf3 Bd6 12 Bxf6 Qxf6 13 Qxf6 gxf6 14 Ne2 Be6 15 b3 a5 16 a4 c5 17 Rad1 Rfd8 18 f4 c4.**

B) <u>4 c3 Nge7 5 Bc4</u> (5 cxd4 d5 6 e5 Bg4) <u>d5 6 exd5 Nxd5 7 0-0 Nb6 8 Bb5 dxc3 9 Nd4 Bd7 10 Bxc6 bxc6 11 Nxc3 Be7</u>.

C) <u>4 Bc4 Bc5 5 c3 Nf6</u> transposes into the Giuoco Piano.

FOUR KNIGHTS GAME

<u>1 e4 e5 2 Nf3 Nc6 3 Nc3 Nf6 4 Bb5</u> (4 d4 exd4 5 Nxd4 Bb4 see Scotch Game, or if 5 Nd5 then Nb4) <u>Bb4 5 0-0 0-0 6 d3 d6 7 Bg5 Bxc3 8 bxc3 Qe7 9 Re1 Nd8 10 d4 Ne6 11 Bc1 c5</u>.

VIENNA GAME

<u>1 e4 e5 2 Nc3 Nf6</u> now,

A) <u>3 Bc4 Nc6 4 d3 Na5 5 Bb3</u> (5 Nge2 Nxc4) <u>Nxb3 6 axb3 d5</u>.

B) <u>3 f4 d5 4 fxe5 Nxe4 5 Nf3</u> (5 Qf3 Nc6) <u>Bg4</u>.

C) <u>3 g3 d5 4 exd5 Nxd5 5 Bg2 Nxc3 6 bxc3 Bd6</u>.

KING'S GAMBIT

<u>1 e4 e5 2 f4 exf4 3 Nf3 d6</u> now,

A) <u>4 Bc4 h6 5 d4 g5 6 h4</u> (6 0-0 Bg7 7 c3 Nc6 8 g3 Bh3) <u>Bg7 7 c3 Nc6 8 Qb3 Qe7 9 0-0 Nf6 10 hxg5 hxg5 11 Nxg5 Nxd4 12 Bxf7+ Kd8 13 cxd4 Nxe4 14 Bxf4 Bxd4+</u>.

B) <u>4 d4 g5 5 h4 g4 6 Ng1</u> (6 Ng5 f6) <u>f3 7 gxf3 Be7 8 h5 Bh4+ 9 Ke2 f5</u>.

CENTER GAME

<u>1 e4 e5 2 d4 exd4 3 Qxd4</u> (3 c3 Ne7) <u>Nc6 4 Qe3 Nf6 5 Nc3 Bb4 6 Bd2 0-0 7 0-0-0 Re8 8 Qg3 Rxe4 9 a3 Bd6 10 f4 Re8 11 Nf3 Bc5 12 Bd3 d5</u>.

COLLE SYSTEM

<u>1 d4 Nf6 2 Nf3 b6 3 e3 Bb7 4 Bd3 e6 5 0-0 c5 6 Nbd2 Nc6 7 c3 d5 8 Re1 Be7 9 dxc5 bxc5 10 e4 0-0 11 exd5 Qxd5</u>.

CATALAN OPENING/IRREGULAR "d" PAWN

<u>1 d4 Nf6 2 c4</u> (2 Bg5 Ne4 3 Bh4 c5 4 f3 g5 5 fxe4 hxg4 6 e3 Bh6 7 Bc4 e6, or if 2 Nf3 b6 3 e3 Bb7 4 Bd3e6 5 Nbd2 c5) <u>e6 3 g3 d5 4 Bg2 dxc4 5 Qa4+ Nbd7 6 Qxc4</u> (6 Nbd2 c6 7 Qxc4 e5) <u>a6 7 Nf3</u> (7 Qc2 c5 6Nf3 b6) <u>b5 8 Qc6 Rb8 9 0-0 Bb7 10 Qc2 c5</u>.

NIMZO-INDIAN DEFENSE

<u>1 d4 Nf6 2 c4 e6 3 Nc3 Bb4</u> now,

A) <u>4 e3 0-0 5 Bd3 d5 6 Nf3 c5 7 0-0 Nc6 8 a3 Bxc3 9 bxc3 dxc4 10 Bxc4 Qc7</u> with the idea of 11 e5.

B) <u>4 a3 Bxc3+ 5 bxc3 c5 6 f3</u> (6 e3 b6) <u>**d5 7 cxd5 Nxd5 8 dxc5**</u> (8 Qd3 cxd4 9 cxd4 Nc6 10 e4 Nb6) <u>**f5 9 e4 fxe4 10 Qc2**</u> (10 fxe4 Qh4+) <u>**e3 11 Bd3 Nd7**</u>.

C) <u>4 Bg5 h6 5 Bh4 c5 6 d5 b5 7 dxe6</u> (7 e4 exd5 8 exd5 0-0 9 Bd3 bxc4 10 Bxc4 Qe8+ 11 Qe2 Ne4) <u>**fxe6 8 cxb5 d5 9 e3 0-0**</u>.

D) <u>4 Qc2 d5 5 a3</u> (5 cxd5 exd5 6 Bg5 h6 7 Bh4 0-0) <u>**Bxc3+ 6 Qxc3 Ne4 7 Qc2 c5 8 dxc5 Nc6 9 cxd5 exd5 10 Nf3 Bf5 11 b4 0-0 12 Bb2 b6 13 b5 bxc5 14 bxc6 Qa5+ 15 Nd2 Rab8 16 Rd1 d4 17 c7 Qxc7 18 Nxe4 Bxe4 19 Qd2 Rfe8**</u>.

QUEEN'S INDIAN DEFENSE

<u>1 d4 Nf6 2 c4 e6 3 Nf3 b6</u> now,

A) <u>4 g3 Bb7 5 Bg2 Be7 6 0-0 0-0 7 Nc3 Ne4 8 Qc2 Nxc3 9 Qxc3 f5 10 b3 Bf6</u>.

B) <u>4 e3 Bb7 5 Bd3 d5 6 0-0 Bd6 7 b3 0-0 8 Bb2 Nbd7 9 Nc3 a6</u>.

C) <u>4 a3 Bb7 5 Nc3 d5 6 cxd5</u> (6 Bg5 Be7 7 e3 0-0 8 Rc1 Ne4 9 Bxe7 Qxe7 10 cxd5 exd5 11 Nxe4 dxe4 12 Nd2 Rc8) <u>**Nxd5 7 Qc2 Nxc3 8 bxc3 c5 9 e4 Nd7 10 Bf4 cxd4 11 cxd4 Rc8**</u>.

ENGLISH OPENING

<u>1 c4 Nf6 2 Nc3 e6</u> now,

A) <u>3 Nf3 Bb4 4 Qc2 0-0 5 a3 Bxc3 6 Qxc3 d6 7 g3 e5</u>.

B) <u>3 e4 d5 4 e5 d4 5 exf6</u> (5 Nce2 Nfd7) <u>**dxc3 6 bxc3**</u> (6 fxg7 cxd2+ 7 Bxd2 Bxg7 8 Qc2 Qf6 9 Bc3 e5) <u>**Qxf6 7 d4**</u> (7 Nf3 e5) <u>**e5 8 Nf3**</u> (8 Qe2 Be7 9 dxe5 Qg6 10 Nf3 0-0 11 Bf4 Nc6, or if 9 Qxe5 Qxe5+ 10 dxe5 Nc6) <u>**exd4 9 Bg5**</u> (9 cxd4 Bb4+ 10 Bd2 Bxd2+ 11 Qxd2 0-0) <u>**Qe6+ 10 Be2 h6 11 Nxd4 Qe5**</u>.

BIRD'S OPENING

<u>1 f4 d5 2 Nf3 Nf6 3 e3 g6 4 Be2 Bg7 5 0-0 0-0 6 d3 c5 7 Qe1 Nc6</u>.

SOLKOLSKY'S OPENING

<u>1 b4 e5 2 Bb2 Bxb4 3 Bxe5 Nf6 4 c4 0-0 5 Nf3</u> (5 e3 d5 6 cxd5 Nxd5 7 Nf3 c5) <u>**Nc6 6 Bb2 d5 7 cxd5 Qxd5**</u>.

GROB'S OPENING

1 g4 e5 2 Bg2 h5 3 gxh5 Qg5 4 Bf3 Qh4 5 d3 c6 6 e4 Nf6 7 Qe2 Nxh5.

KING'S INDIAN ATTACK

1 Nf3 Nf6 2 g3 b6 3 Bg2 Bb7 4 0-0 e6 5 d3 d5 6 Nbd2 Be7 7 Re1 c5 8 e4 Nc6 9 e5 Nd7 10 Nf1 Qc7 11 Qe2 h6 12 h4 0-0-0.

Pattern Recognition—
The Key to Learning Tactics

Although the opening is important in setting the stage for battle, most scholastic players win or lose the majority of their games in the tactical skirmishes. Pattern recognition is the key element in being able to effectively understand tactics.

To improve your tactical ability you need to observe and analyze common tactical patterns that occur in practical play. Playing games will help, but this is trial and error learning, a slow process. In order to speed things up you can get help from your instructor, books, and databases to provide you with tactical problems for study.

There are numerous books that provide excellent positions with common tactical themes. A good book to start with is *The Art of the Checkmate* by Renaud and Kahn (New York: Dover, 1962). This book analyzes the important checkmating patterns you will find in practical play. Unfortunately, it is available only in English descriptive notation. *Winning Chess Tactics for Juniors* by Lou Hays (Park Hill, OK: Hays Publishing, 1994) has 534 basic tactical problems taken from the more comprehensive book *Combination Challenge* by Lou Hays (Dallas: Hays Publishing, 1991), which has 1,154 tactical problems to solve. Intermediate and advanced players should get *Combina-*

tion Challenge. Two other excellent books with many tactical positions (also in English descriptive notation) are *1001 Winning Chess Sacrifices and Combinations* and *1001 Brilliant Ways to Checkmate* by Fred Reinfeld (Hollywood, CA: Wilshire Book Company, 1955). All of these books present diagrams in a problem format. The answers are given in the back.

When studying these books, start at the beginning. Spend no more than five minutes on any one problem. If you feel that you have found the solution within the five minutes look up the answer in the back to verfify your solution. Make a note of which problems you were unable to solve. When you reach the end of the book, start over again, going over just the problems you missed. If you miss the same problem again, make another note, move on, and repeat the process until you know the solution to every problem.

Two excellent books on positional play that I recommend for intermediate or advanced players are *My System* by Aron Nimzowitsch, algebraic edition (Dallas: Hays Publishing, 1991) and *Chess Praxis* by Nimzowitsch, algebraic edition (Dallas: Hays Publishing, 1993). And one of the best books ever written on how to attack is *Art of Attack in Chess* by Vladimir Vukovic, algebraic edition (London: Everyman, 1998). This book is highly recommended for intermediate and advanced players. Finally, an old classic has just been republished in algebraic format. It is *The Middlegame in Chess* by Reuben Fine (New York: Random House, 2003). The first 167 pages deal with tactics and the rest deals with positional advantages.

The following tactical situations are taken from positions I use in my lessons with intermediate and advanced students. I will not repeat anything that has already been presented in my previous two books. When I get to problems for you to solve I will first give an extremely simplified example of a tactical pattern. Then the follow-up diagram will use this theme in a more complicated position, which will require you to find the moves to set up the combination.

I will begin by using three variations of the Philidor's Defense taken from several games I played in simultaneous exhibitions. They all take advantage of the weak "f7" square.

PHILIDOR'S DEFENSE GAME #1

1 e4 e5 2 Nf3 d6

This move initiates Philidor's Defense, which is now rarely seen in master play. Black subjects himself to a cramped game by blocking his Bishop on "f8".

3 d4

White boldly takes a foothold in the center and threatens Black's "e" Pawn.

3...Nd7

It would have been stronger to play 3...Nf6 attacking White's "e" Pawn.

4 Bc4

White develops his Bishop, putting immediate pressure on Black's weak "f7" Pawn.

4...Nf6?

Diagram 11. Position after 4...Nf6.

Black should have played 4...c6, after which the game might have continued 5 0-0 Be7 6 dxe5 dxe5 7 Ng5 Bxg5 8 Qh5 Qe7 9 Qxg5 Qxg5 10 Bxg5. White still stands better as he has the Bishop pair, a lead in development, and more space.

See if you can find White's best move in Diagram 11 without looking at the next move in the game. Remember that in some way White will take advantage of Black's weak Pawn on "f7".

5 dxe5!

This opens up White's Queen on the "d" file, which you will soon see plays a vital role. It was possible to win a Pawn with 5 Ng5 d5. However, after either 6 exd5 Bd6 or 6 Bxd5 Nxd5 7 exd5 Be7 Black's active pieces give him some compensation for the Pawn.

5...Nxe5

If Black played 5...dxe5 he would have had no way of defending his "f" Pawn after 6 Ng5!.

6 Nxe5 dxe5 7 Bxf7+

White takes advantage of Black's King being an overworked defender, where he is defending both the Queen and Pawn on "f7".

7...Kxf7

At a glance this may appear to be a horrible blunder, which loses a Queen. However, Black sees that he has a way to recover his Queen.

8 Qxd8 Bb4+ 9 Qd2 Bxd2+ 10 Nxd2

White is a Pawn ahead and eventually won the game.

PHILIDOR'S DEFENSE GAME #2

1 e4 e5 2 Nf3 d6 3 d4 Nd7 4 Bc4 Be7?

Diagram 12. Position after 4...Be7

White can force the win of at least a Pawn. See if you can find White's next move without looking at the next move in the game.

5 dxe5!

Once again opening up "d" file for the Queen will allow White to take advantage of Black's weakness on "f7".

5...Nxe5

See if you can find the move that would win at least a minor piece for White if Black played 5...dxe5?.

The answer is 6 Qd5! threatening 7 Qxf7++. If Black defends the Pawn on "f7" with 6... Nh6 White would be a piece ahead after 7 Bxh6 0-0 8 Be3.

6 Nxe5 dxe5

See if you can find White's move here that wins at least a Pawn without looking at the next move in the game.

7 Qh5

White threatens Black's Pawns on "f7" and "e5".

7...g6 8 Qxe5 Nf6 9 Bh6

White is a Pawn ahead, has prevented the Black King from castling Kingside, and threatens 10 Bg7. White eventually won the game.

PHILIDOR'S DEFENSE GAME #3

1 e4 e5 2 Nf3 d6 3 d4 Nd7 4 Bc4 exd4 5 Nxd4 Be7??

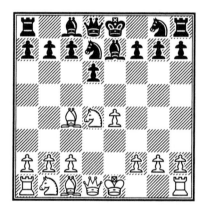

Diagram 13. Position after 5…Be7

This quiet developing move will lose Black's Queen. It would have been better to first develop his Knight with 5…Ngf6.

See if you can find White's best move in Diagram 13 without looking at the next move in the game.

6 Bxf7 +!

Again taking advantage of the weak "f7" square. Black's King is exposed to attack.

6...Kxf7

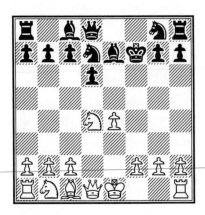

Diagram 14. Position after 6...Bxf7

Black's only other legal move, 6...Kf8, would immediately lose his Queen after 7 Ne6+.

Black's King has now been exposed. Without looking at the next move in the game, see if you can find White's move, which will lead to the win of Black's Queen.

7 Ne6!

I have had students rated over 2200 who had difficulty finding this move! Many of my students think they have trapped Black's Queen after 7 Qh5+ g6 8 Qd5+ Ke8 9 Ne6. This is a fine example of the *inert image*. Students often analyze only to move eight, thinking Black's Queen is trapped and it is all over. However, Black can play either 9...Nb6 or 9...Ndf6, which frees his Queen and leaves him a piece ahead.

With the text move White attacks Black's Queen and "c" Pawn, sinking his Knight deep into enemy territory. This will end up winning Black's Queen!

7...Qe8

Black cannot capture the Knight with 7...Kxe6?? because of 8 Qd5+ Kf6 9 Qf5++.

8 Nxc7 Qf8 9 Qh5+ g6 10 Qd5+ Kf6 11 Bg5+ Kg7 12 Ne6+

Black loses his Queen on the next move.

TACTICAL PROBLEMS TO WORK ON

The following segment will cover some important tactical problems for you to use as training exercises. These are typical problems I provide my students for study that haven't already appeared in my earlier books, *Chess for Juniors* and *Unbeatable Chess Lessons for Juniors*. Use a sheet of paper to cover up the answers just below each diagram. If you haven't figured out the solution to any one problem within five minutes, look at the answer, make a note of it, and move on to the next problem.

CHECKMATE THEMES

I have used the common pattern found in Diagrams 15 & 16 numerous times in actual play. It will eventually come up in some of your games.

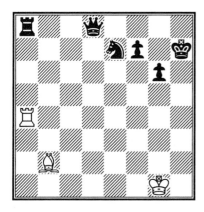

Diagram 15. White to move and mate in two moves.

Answer: White forces mate in two moves with **1 Rh4+ Kg8 2 Rh8++**.

You simply need to remember the pattern in Diagram 15 and build on it to find the solution to the problem in Diagram 16.

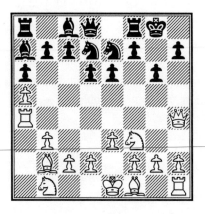

Diagram 16. White to move and mate in three moves.

Answer: White forces mate in three moves beginning with a clearance sacrifice, **1 Qxh7+ Kxh7 2 Rh4+ Kg8 3 Rh8++**.

In Diagram 17 a couple of small changes have been made. White's Rook is on "a1" instead of "a4" and White's Bishop is on "d3" instead of "f1". You will see that a couple of small changes can completely change the solution to finding the best move in a position.

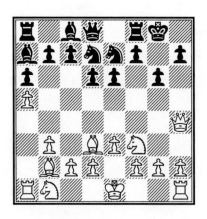

Diagram 17. White to move and mate in four moves.

Answer: White begins by bringing his Knight into play and threatening mate on "h7" with **1 Ng5**. Black's best practical try to prevent mate is **1...h5**. Now look again. Do you see White's awesome move that forces mate in three more moves? Here is the solution, **2 Qxh5!** (White now threatens both 3 Qh7++ and 3 Qh8++) **Nf6** (this was the only move to delay the mate, if 2...gxh5 then 3 Bh7++) **3 Bxf6 gxh5 4 Bh7++**.

In Diagram 18 a pin makes a back-rank mate possible for White in two moves.

Diagram 18. White to move and mate in two moves.

Answer: **1 Re8+ Rxe8 2 Rxe8++**. Now that you have seen this pattern you should be able to apply it to a slightly more complicated situation.

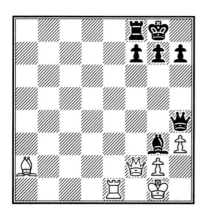

Diagram 19. White to move and mate in two moves.

Answer: **1 Qxf7+! Rxf7** (if 1...Kh8 then 2 Qxf8++) **2 Re8++.**

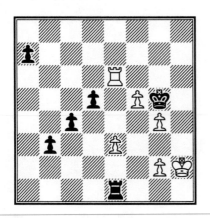

Diagram 20. White to move and mate in two moves.

Answer: 1 Rg6+ Kh4 2 g3++.

Without having seen the pattern in Diagram 20, finding the solution to the problem in Diagram 21 would be more difficult. Let's see how fast you can solve the next problem.

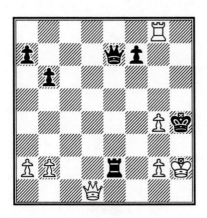

Diagram 21. Ståhlberg versus Becker, 1946. White to move and mate in two moves.

Answer: 1 Qe1+! Rxe1 2 g3++.

In Diagram 22 we have an important pattern, which is very common in practical play.

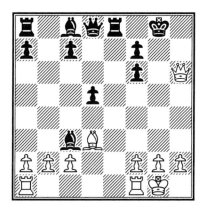

Diagram 22. White to move and mate in four moves.

Answer: 1 Bh7+ Kh8 2 Bg6+ Kg8 3 Qh7+ Kf8 4 Qxf7++.

Now you must think deeply as you will need to set up the pattern found in Diagram 22 in the next problem.

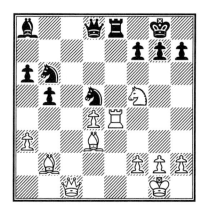

Diagram 23. Horowitz versus Kevitz, New York, 1931. White to move and mate in seven moves.

Answer: 1 Qg5! (threatening 2 Qxg7++) **g6** (not 1...Qxg5?? because of 2 Rxe8++) **2 Qh6 gxf5 3 Rg4+! fxg4 4 Bxh7+ Kh8 5 Bg6+ Kg8 6 Qh7+ Kf8 7 Qxf7++.**

In Diagram 24 White forces a quick win using numerous tactical themes, which include a discovered attack, cutting communication between pieces, and a back-rank mate threat.

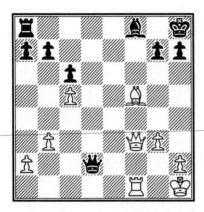

Diagram 24. White to move and win.

Answer: 1 Bc8!. Black loses quickly because of White's threat of 2 Qxf8++.

Diagram 25 takes the themes used in the previous diagram just one step further. White now needs to include the use of a "*zwischenzug*" (a German chess term meaning "*in-between move*").

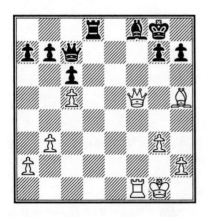

Diagram 25. Réti versus Bogoljubow, New York, 1924. White to move and win.

Answer: 1 Bf7+! (this forces Black's King to move away from the defense of his Bishop) **Kh8 2 Be8!**. Again, Black loses quickly because of White's threat of 3 Qxf8+.

In Diagram 26 we have a typical forced mate due to penetration along an open "h" file. However, White must prevent Black's King from escaping through "f7".

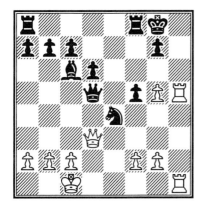

Diagram 26. White to move and mate in two moves.

Answer: **1 g6 Qxd3** (or any move for Black) **2 Rh8++**.

Now with some slight changes to Diagram 26 we reach Diagram 27. The same general pattern is still going to be used, but White is required to use a more elaborate technique.

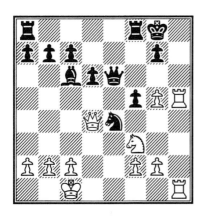

Diagram 27. Alekhine versus Mindeno, Simultaneous Exhibition, Holland, 1933. White to move and win.

Answer: **1 Ne5!**. White immediately cuts off Black's King from escaping through "f7". If White played an immediate 1 g6 then Black would simply win the Pawn with 1...Qxg6. After 1 Ne5! if **1...Qxe5 2 g6!** (threatening 3 Rh8++) **Qf4+ 3 Qe3 Qh6 4 Rxh6 gxh6 5 Qxh6** followed by **6 Qh8++**. Or if **1...dxe5 2 g6! Qxg6 3 Qc4+** and when Black eventually interposes on "f7" White plays **Rh8++**.

In the next two diagrams we find similar patterns using variations of *"Boden's Mate."*

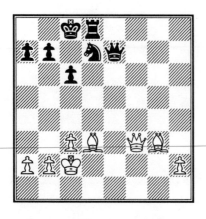

Diagram 28. White to move and mate in two moves.

Answer: 1 Qxc6+! bxc6 2 Ba6++.

Diagram 29. Ward versus Browne, Nottingham, 1874. White to move and mate in three.

Answer: 1 Qxf6+ gxf6 2 Bh6+ Qg7 3 Rxf6++.

In the following two diagrams we have another very common pattern known as *"Anastasia's Mate."*

Diagram 30. White to move and mate in two moves.

Answer: 1 Qxh7+ Kxh7 2 Rh1++.

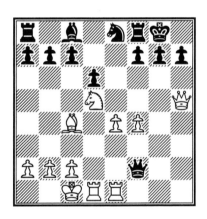

Diagram 31. White to move and mate in five moves.

Answer: 1 Ne7+ Kh8 2 Qxh7+! Kxh7 3 Rh1+ Bh3 4 Rxh3+ Qh4 5 Rxh4++.

The following position was reached after Black had just played Rd3??. Black in his overconfidence played aggressively and abandoned the protection of his first rank. This proved to be a fatal mistake.

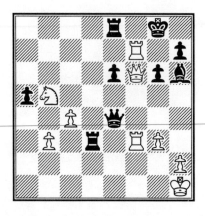

Diagram 32. Snyder versus Dahlberg, Santa Monica, 1971. White to move and mate in four moves.

Answer: 1 Rg7+!. Black sat there and stared at the position for several minutes in disbelief. He then resigned. There is no way to avoid mate. If **1...Bxg7** (or if 1...Kh8 2 Rxg6+ Bg7 3 Qxg7++) **2 Qf7+ Kh8 3 Qxe8+ Bf8 4 Qxf8++.**

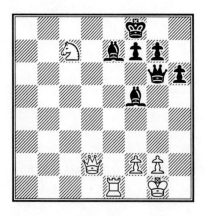

Diagram 33. White to move and mate in two moves.

Answer: 1 Qd8+ Bxd8 2 Re8++.

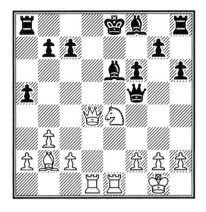

Diagram 34. Pollock versus Allies, Buffalo, 1893. White to move and mate in five.

Answer: 1 Qd7+! Bxd7 2 Nd6+ Kd8 3 Nf7+ Kc8 4 Re8+ Bxe8 5 Rd8++.

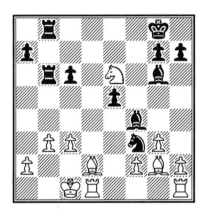

Diagram 35. Black to move and mate in three moves.

Answer: 1...Rxb3! 2 axb3 Rxb3 followed by 3...Rb1++.

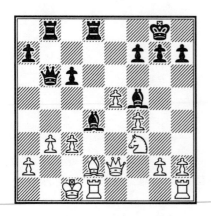

Diagram 36. Rosanes versus Anderssen, Breslau, 1862. Black to move and mate in five.

Answer: 1...Qxb3! 2 axb3 Rxb3 3 Be1. This was the move actually played in the game. It gave White the best practical chance because it forced Black to find the brilliant winning continuation from here. White could have delayed the game one more move by giving up his Queen with 3 Qe4 Bxe4 4 Be1 Be3+ 5 Nd2 Rb1++. However, this would have been simple for Black to find. After 3 Be1 the game concluded **3...Be3+! 4 Qxe3 Rb1++**.

In the following two diagrams we have examples of *"Greco's Mate,"* another very important pattern to know.

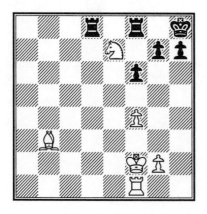

Diagram 37. White to move and mate in two.

Answer: 1 Ng6 + hxg6 2 Rh1++.

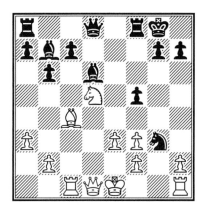

Diagram 38. Johnston versus Marshall, Chicago, 1899. White to move and mate in four.

Answer: 1 Ne7+ Kh8 2 Ng6+ hxg6 3 hxg3+ Qh4 4 Rxh4++.

In the following three positions we have examples of the *"Smothered Mate,"* which is where a King is surrounded by his own pieces and a Knight delivers the mate!

In Diagram 39 White was greedy and just captured Black's Bishop on "b4" with his "a" Pawn—a trap in the Budapest Gambit reached after **1 d4 Nf6 2 c4 e5 3 dxe5 Ng4 4 Nf3 Nc6 5 Bf4 Bb4+ 6 Nbd2 Qe7 7 a3 Ngxe5 8 axb4??**

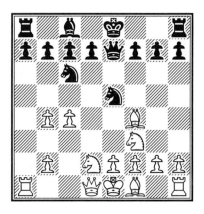

Diagram 39. Position after 8 axb4. Black to move and mate in one move.

Answer: 8...Nd3++.

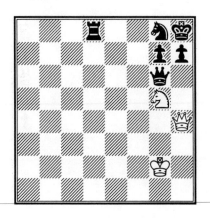

Diagram 40. Damiano, 1512. White to move and mate in two moves.

Answer: 1 Qxh7+! Qxh7 2 Nf7++.

In Diagram 41 we have a variation of the famous smothered mate known as *"Philidor's Legacy."*

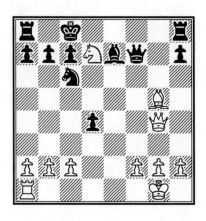

Diagram 41. Morphy versus Amateur, Paris, 1859. White to move and mate in three.

Answer: 1 Nb6+ Kb8 2 Qc8+! Rxc8 3 Nd7++.

In the following three positions we have common patterns, forcing mate through the coordination of a Knight and Bishop.

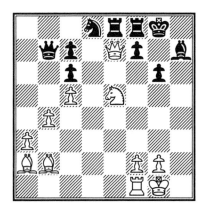

Diagram 42. White to move and mate in two moves.

Answer: 1 Ng4! Rxe7 (or any move) **2 Nh6++**.

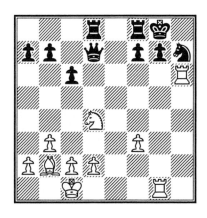

Diagram 43. Aspscheneek versus Amateur, Riga, 1934. White to move and mate in four moves.

Answer: 1 Rxg7+! Kxg7 2 Nf5+ Kg8 3 Rg6+! fxg6 4 Nh6++.

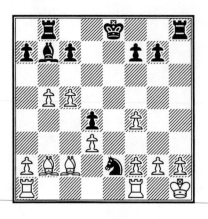

Diagram 44. Black to move and mate in three moves.

Answer: 1...Ke7! 2 Rfe1 (2 h3 Rxh3++) Rxh2+ 3 Kxh2 Rh8++.

In the following two positions we have common patterns, forcing mate through the coordination of two Bishops.

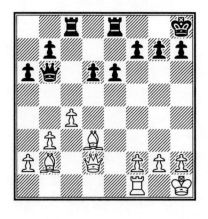

Diagram 45. White to move and mate in two moves.

Answer: 1 Qh6 (threatening 2 Qxg7++ or 2 Qxh7++) f5 2 Qxg7++.

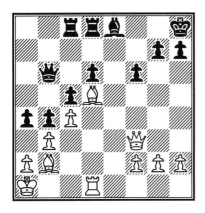

Diagram 46. White to move and mate in two moves.

Answer: **1 Qxf6!** (threatening 2 Qxg7++ or 2 Qf8++) **gxf6 2 Bxf6++**.

In the following two positions we have common patterns, forcing mate through the coordination of two Knights.

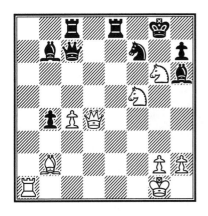

Diagram 47. White to move and mate in two moves.

Answer: **1 Qh8+! Nxh8 2 Nxh6++**.

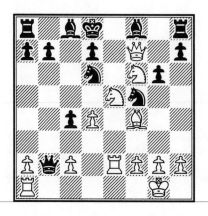

Diagram 48. White to move and mate in three moves.

Answer: **1 Qe8 + Kc7** (if 1...Nxe8 then 2 Nf7++) **2 Nd5+ Kb8 3 Nxd7++.**

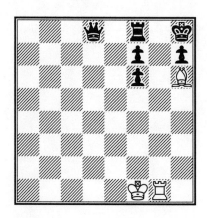

Diagram 49. White to move and mate in two moves.

Answer: **1 Bg7+ Kg8 2 Bxf6++.**

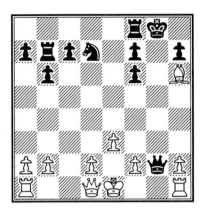

Diagram 50. White to move and win.

Answer: 1 **Qf3!**. White is now attacking Black's Queen and Rook on "b7". If 1...**Qxf3 2 Rg1+ Kh8 3 Bg7+ Kg8 4 Bxf6+ Qg4 5 Rxg4++**.

In the following two positions we have examples of *"Anderssen's Mate."*

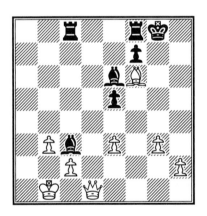

Diagram 51. White to move and mate in two moves.

Answer: 1 **Qh5 Ra8** (or any Black move) 2 **Qh8++**.

Diagram 52. White to move and mate in three moves.

Answer: 1 Bxh7+ Kxh7 2 Qh5+ Kg8 3 Qh8++.

In the following four positions we have sacrifices that expose a castled King to a mating attack.

Diagram 53. Black to move and mate in three moves.

Answer: 1...Rxg2+ 2 Kxg2 Rg8+ 3 Kh1 Qf3++.

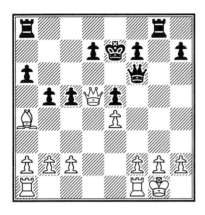

Diagram 54. Katalymov versus Bazarov, St. Petersburg, 1905. Black to move and mate in six moves.

Answer: **1...Rxg2+ 2 Kh1** (if 2 Kxg2 then 2...Rg8+ 3 Kh1 Qf3++ or if 3 Kh3 then 3...Qh6++) **Rxh2+ 3 Kxh2** (if 3 Kg1 then 3...Rg8+ 4 Kxh2 Qh4++) **Qh4+ 4 Kg2 Qg4+ 5 Kh2 Qh5+ 6 Kg2 Rg8++**.

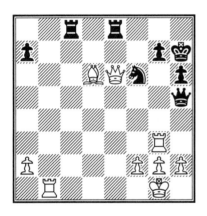

Diagram 55. Chigorin versus Bird, New York, 1889. White to move and win.

Answer: White began his long King hunt with **1 Rxg7+! Kxg7 2 Rb7+ Kg6 3 Qf7+ Kf5 4 Rb5+ Ke4 5 f3+** and Black gets mated in all variations or White could simply win Black's Queen. The game concluded with **5...Ke3** (5...Kd3 might have continued 6 Qb3+ Rc3 7 Qd1+ Ke3 and White has the choice of winning Black's Queen with 8 Rxh5 or trapping Black's King and going for mate with 8 Rb4 Qf5 9 Qd4+ Ke2 10 Qxc3 Qg5 11 Rb2+ Kd1 12 Qd3+ Ke1 13 Qf1++) **6 Qb3+ Ke2 7 Qb2+ Kd3 8 Qb1+ Ke2** (8...Rc2 would have lasted a little longer after 9 Qd1+ Rd2 10 Qb3+ Ke2 11 Qc4+ Rd3 12 Rb2+ Ke1 13 Bg3+ Kd1 14 Qc2++) **9 Rb2+ Ke3 10 Qe1+ Kd4 11 Qd2+ Kc4 12 Rb4++**.

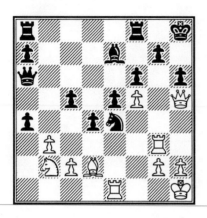

Diagram 56. Alexander versus Clarke, Leicester, 1960. White to move and win.

Answer: White cracked open Black's castled King position with **1 Rxg7!** (threatening 2 Qxh6++) **Kxg7 2 Bxh6+ Kh8** (if 2...Kg8 or 2...Kh7 then 3 Qg6+ Kh8 4 Qg7++) **3 Bxf8+ Kg8 4 Bxe7** and Black's King will not last for long.

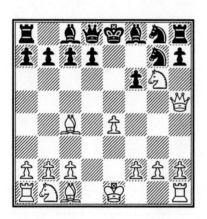

Diagram 57. Fritz versus Amateur, Germany, 1880s. White to move and mate in seven moves.

Answer: 1 Bf7+! Kxf7 2 Ne5+ Ke6 3 Qf7+ Kd6 (if 3...Kxe5, then 4 Qd5++) **4 Nc4+ Kc5** (if 4...Kc6 then 5 Qd5++) **5 Qd5+ Kb4 6 a3+** (this is fun since we have other mates in two moves such as 6 Bd2+ Ka4 7 b3++, 6 c3+ Ka4 7 b3++, and the subtle moves that don't attack the King but still force a mate are the coolest of all, such as 6 Nc3 followed by 7 a3++, or 6 a4 followed by 7 Bd2++) **Ka4 7 b3++.**

The great American player Paul Morphy composed the following endgame mate problem during the mid 1800s, using the idea of "*zugzwang*" (this German term is used to describe a situation where a player whose turn it is to move would rather pass because any move made is harmful).

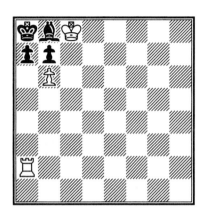

Diagram 58. Problem by Morphy. White to move and mate in two moves.

Answer: 1 Ra6! bxa6 (if Black moves his Bishop, i.e. 1...Bd6, then 2 Rxa7++) **2 b7++.**

The following three positions I set up for my students to be sure they remember all possible legal moves in a situation.

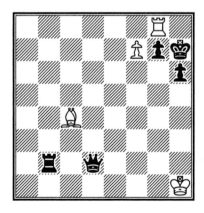

Diagram 59. What is White's best possible move?

Answer: 1 f8=N++!. The idea of *under promotion* is often overlooked. Under promotion can sometimes be an advantage. By not promoting a piece into a Queen you may avoid stalemating your opponent or, because of the unique movement of the Knight, either a checkmate or fork may be available to you.

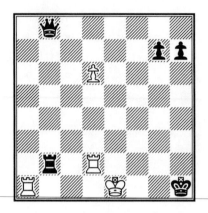

Diagram 60. What is White's best possible move?

Answer: 1 0-0-0++!. Players sometimes forget about castling late in the game. Some players forget that when you castle Queenside that your Rook can pass over the "b1" square if it is attacked.

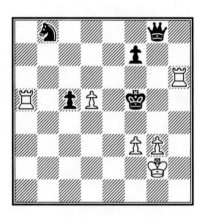

Diagram 61. What is White's best possible move?

Answer: 1 dxc6++!. The only possible checkmate is if Black had just moved his Pawn from "c7" to "c5" allowing *"en passant"* capture as in this case. Even more advanced players sometimes forget about this special rule!

I often set up this position because it is tricky to the eye.

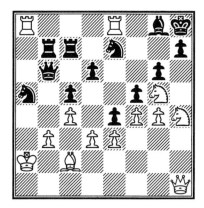

Diagram 62. What is White's best move?

Answer: **1 Qa1++!** It is easy to overlook the long-range powers of the Queen (or even Bishops and Rooks) on long open ranks and diagonals. Always keep your eyes open!

THEMES INVOLVING THE WIN OF MATERIAL

Many of these problems will contain elements of more than one tactical pattern. However, in most cases a common theme will be involved within the focus of a group of problems.

One of the most common ways to win material is *"removing the guard."* An important defending piece is eliminated, undermining the protection of another piece or critical square. The following ten positions use this pattern to win material.

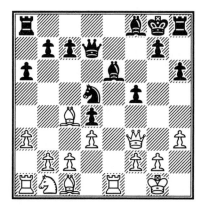

Diagram 63. What is White's best move?

Answer: White immediately removes the protection of Black's Knight and wins a Bishop with **1 Rxe6!**. Black cannot recapture with **1...Qxe6** as **2 Bxd5** pins and wins Black's Queen.

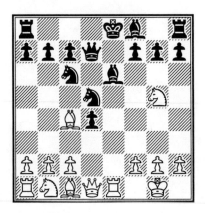

Diagram 64. What is White's best move?

Answer: White exposes Black's King to attack with **1 Nxf7! Kxf7** (not 1...Qxf7 because of 2 Bxd5) **2 Qf3+ Kg8** (other moves lose quickly, i.e., 2...Kg6 3 Rxe6+ and if 3...Nf6 then 4 Qe4+ Kh5 5 Be2+ Ng4 6 Qxg4++, or if 3...Qxe6 then 4 Bd3+ Qf5 5 Qxf5++) **3 Rxe6! Rd8** (Black is unable to recapture with 3...Qxe6 because of 4 Qxd5! with mate to soon follow—also if 3...Ncb4 then 4 Re4 Nxc2? 5 Re8!) **4 Qe4** with a great position for White.

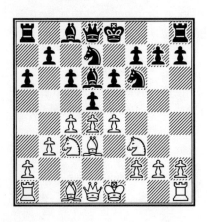

Diagram 65. Loftsson versus Batchelder, Newport Beach, 1974. What is Black's best move?

Answer: Black won a piece after **1...Bb4 2 Bd2 Bxc3 3 Bxc3 dxe4**.

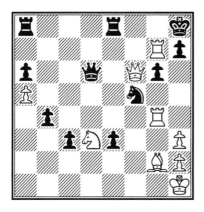

Diagram 66. What is White's best move?

Answer: 1 Rh4! (threatening 2 Rhxh7++). Now to avoid a quick mate Black has nothing better than to give up his Queen with **1...Nxg7** (if either 1...Nxh4 or 1...h6 then 2 Qf7! forces mate, or if 1...h5 then 2 Rxg6+ Qxf6 3 Rxh5+ Nh6 4 Rhxh6++) **2 Qxd6**.

The position in Diagram 67 was reached after **1 e4 e5 2 Nf3 Nc6 3 Bb5 a6 4 Bxc6 dxc6 5 0-0 Bg4 6 h3 h5 7 d3 Qf6 8 Bg5??**. White has just made one of the most common tactical blunders by attacking a Queen with a Bishop that is defended by a Knight that is pinned to a Queen by a Bishop! This long, strung-out sentence is funny, but it's true! Sometimes my students will say, "Say that again, but slowly this time." This allows Black to win a piece.

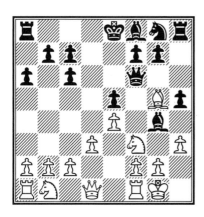

Diagram 67. What is Black's best move?

Answer: 8...Bxf3. Black removes the defender of White's Bishop on g5. As a result White must lose a minor piece. If **9 Bxf6** (or if 9 Qxf3 then 9...Qxg5) **Bxd1 10 Bxg7 Bxg7 11 Rxd1**.

In Diagram 68 we have the same type of pattern found in Diagram 67. The position was reached after **1 e4 e5 2 Nf3 Nc6 3 d4 exd4 4 Nxd4 Nf6 5 Nc3 Bb4 6 Nxc6 bxc6 7 Bd3 d5 8 exd5 cxd5 9 0-0 0-0 10 Bg5 c6 11 Qf3 Bg4??**.

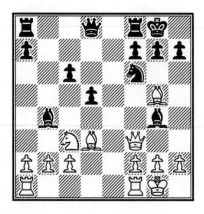

Diagram 68. What is White's best move?

Answer: 12 Bxf6. Black must lose a minor piece. If **12...Bxf3** (if 12...Qxf6, then 13 Qxg4) then **13 Bxd8 Rfxd8 14 gxf3**.

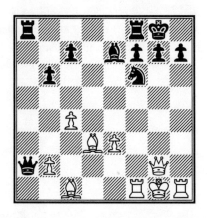

Diagram 69. What is White's best move?

Answer: White removes the critical defender of Black's "h" Pawn with **1 Rxf6!**. If **1...Bxf6** mate soon follows after **2 Bxh7+ Kh8 3 Bb1+ Kg8 4 Rh8+! Kxh8 5 Qh2+ Bh4 6 Qxh4+ Kg8 7 Qh7++**.

In the next position the idea of removing the guard of a critical square is illustrated.

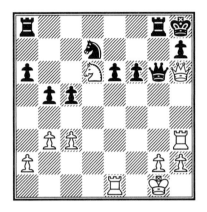

Diagram 70. Snyder versus Maki, Santa Monica, 1974. What is White's best move?

Answer: **1 Rg3!**. Black must lose his Queen as he cannot lose control of the critical "f7" square to win White's Queen with **1...Qxh6** because of **2 Nf7++**.

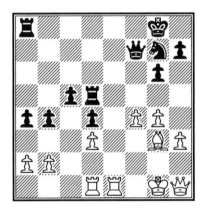

Diagram 71. What is White's best move?

Answer: White plays **1 Re7!**. This leaves Black with the choice of losing his Queen or allowing a killer fork after **1...Qxe7 2 Qxd5+** followed by **3 Qxa8+**.

The following is an awesome illustration of the idea of removing the guard. It requires you to keep on finding one brilliant move after another using this same idea!

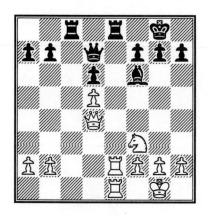

Diagram 72. Adams versus Torre, New Orleans, 1924. What is White's best move?

Answer: 1 Qg4! (White threatens Black's unprotected Queen) **Qb5** (Black cannot capture White's Queen with 1...Qxg4 because of 2 Rxe8+ Rxe8 3 Rxe8++) **2 Qc4!** (White threatens Black's unprotected Queen again!) **Qd7** (once again Black cannot capture Black's Queen with either 2...Qxc4 or 2...Rxc4 as 3 Rxe8+ leads to mate) **3 Qc7!** (this seems to be a never ending story with the same theme constantly repeated—again Black's Queen is threatened and White's Queen cannot be captured due to mate on "e8") **Qb5** (Black's Queen seems to lead the life of a yo-yo going from "d7" to "b5" and back again, but this will not last for long!) **4 a4! Qxa4 5 Re4! Qb5** (Black does his best to keep his Rook on "e8" protected by the Queen) **6 Qxb7!** and Black resigned. His Queen has run out of squares to move to and still keep his Rook on "e8" protected. If **6...a6** then simply **7 Qxb5** does the trick.

We will now look at a couple of positions that involve the use of the *"Classic Bishop Sacrifice."*

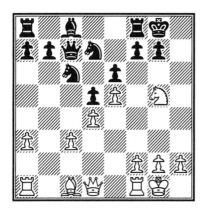

Diagram 73. What is White's best move?

Answer: White forces mate after **1 Qh5** (threatening 2 Qh7++) **Rd8 2 Qxf7+ Kh8 3 Qh5+ Kg8 4 Qh7+ Kf8 5 Qh8+ Ke7 6 Qxg7+ Ke8 7 Qf7++**.

Keeping the winning idea in mind from Diagram 73, now find White's best move in Diagram 74, which is reached after **1 e4 e6 2 d4 d5 3 Nc3 Nf6 4 Bg5 Be7 5 e5 Nfd7 6 Bxe7 Qxe7 7 f4 0-0 8 Nf3 c5 9 dxc5 Nc6 10 Bd3 Qxc5?**.

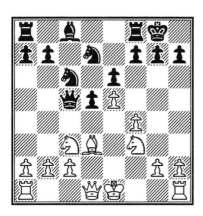

Diagram 74. What is White's best move?

Answer: White uses the Classic Bishop Sacrifice to expose Black's King to a deadly attack beginning with **11 Bxh7+!**. Black would do best to decline the sacrifice with **11...Kh8**. However after **12 Bd3** White is a Pawn ahead. Therefore, let's take a look at what would happen if Black accepts the sacrifice after **11 Bxh7+ Kxh7 12 Ng5+**. Now trying to hide the King with **12...Kg8** loses quickly after **13 Qh5 Rd8 14 Qxf7+ Kh8 15 Qh5+ Kg8 16 Qh7+ Kf8 17 Qh8+ Ke7 18 Qxg7+ Ke8 19 Qf7++**. If Black brings out his King with **12...Kg6** then White continues with **13 Qd3+ f5 14 exf6+ e.p. Kxf6** (if 14...Kh5 then 15 Qh7+ Kg4 16 Ne2 threatening 17 Qh3+) **15 Nce4+ dxe4 16 Nxe4+ Kf7 17 Nxc5 Nxc5 18 Qf3 Kg8 19 0-0-0** and White's Queen, two Pawns, and superior position against Black's three minor pieces should prevail.

We will examine a variety of positions where the use of a *"fork"* or *"double attack"* is the main theme.

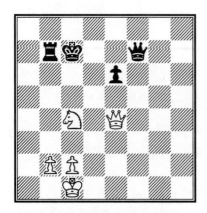

Diagram 75. What is White's best move?

Answer: White wins a Rook after **1 Qxb7+ Kxb7 2 Nd6+ Kc6 3 Nxf7**.

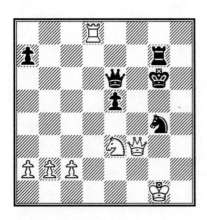

Diagram 76. What is White's best move?

Answer: 1 Rd6! (not 1 Nxg4? because of 1...Qb6+ forking King and Rook) **Qxd6 2 Qxg4+ Kh7 3 Qxg7+ Kxg7 4 Nf5+ Kf6 5 Nxd6**.

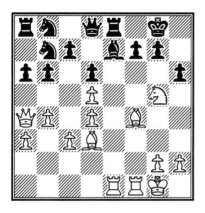

Diagram 77. Kislov versus Victorov, Voronezh, 1971. What is White's best move?

Answer: **1 Bh7+**. Now Black has a choice of **1...Kh8** allowing **2 Nxf7+** forking King and Queen, or **1...Kf8 2 Ne6+! fxe6 3 Bxd6++**.

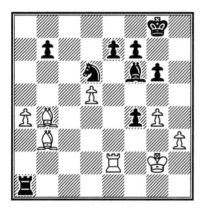

Diagram 78. Rosetto versus Sherwin, Portoroz, 1958. What is Black's best move?

Answer: Black uses a skewer, which only works due to a zwischenzug using a sacrificial Pawn fork. **1...Rb1! 2 Bxd6** (this move almost saves the piece, except for Black's next move) **f3+! 3 Kxf3 Rxb3+ 4 Kg2 exd6**. Black has won a piece.

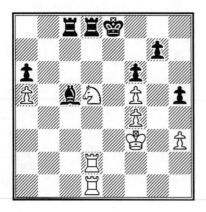

Diagram 79. What is White's best move?

Answer: 1 Nc7+! Ke7 (if 1...Rxc7 then 2 Rxd8+) **2 Rxd8 Rxd8** (2...Rxc7 would last longer) **3 Rxd8 Kxd8 4 Ne6+ Kd7 5 Nxc5+.**

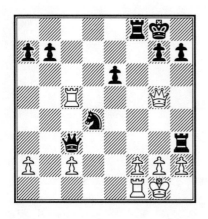

Diagram 80. Levitsky versus Marshall, Breslau, 1912. What is Black's best move?

Answer: Black has a variety of ways to win. However, Black's strongest move is **1...Qg3!** (threatening 2...Qxh2++) **2 Qxg3** (if 2 hxg3 then 2...Ne2++, or if 2 fxg3 Ne2+ 3 Kh1 Rxf1++) **Ne2+ 3 Kh1 Nxg3+ 4 Kg1 Ne2+.**

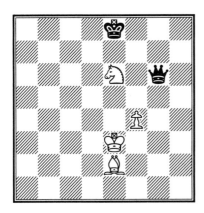

Diagram 81. What is White's best move?

Answer: 1 Bh5! Qxh5 2 Ng7+ Kf7 3 Nxh5.

Diagram 82. Kraus versus Costin, Correspondence , 1914. What is White's best move?

Answer: **1 b4 Qc6 2 Bb5** and White wins Black's Queen. If **2...Qxb5** then **3 Nc7+** followed by **4 Nxb5**.

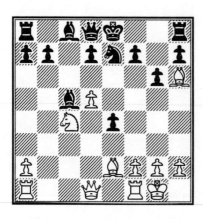

Diagram 83. What is White's best move?

Answer: **1 Qd4!** White forks Black's unprotected Bishop and Rook resulting in the win of a piece. Black cannot play **1...Bxd4??** because of **2 Nd6++**.

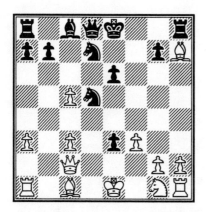

Diagram 84. What is Black's best move?

Answer: Black wins White's Bishop with a Queen flank fork after **1...Qh4+ 2 g3 Qxh7**.

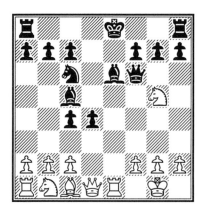

Diagram 85. What is White's best move?

Answer: White wins a piece with **1 Nxe6 fxe6 2 Qh5+ Qf7 3 Qxc5**.

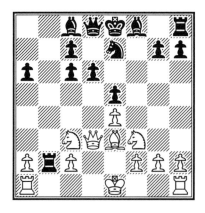

Diagram 86. Feuer versus O'Kelly, Liege, 1934. What is White's best move?

Answer: White recovered his Pawn with a superior position after **1 Nxe5!**. Black cannot capture the Knight with **1...dxe5??** because of **2 Qxd8+ Kxd8 3 0-0-0+** followed by **4 Kxb2**. Therefore, it would be better to meet **1 Nxe5!** with **1...Be6 2 Nf3**. White could have also recovered his Pawn with 1 0-0-0 Rb8 2 Nxe5 Be6. However, White's King is somewhat exposed on the Queenside with the Queens still on the board.

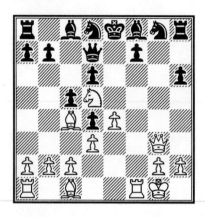

Diagram 87. What is White's best move?

Answer: White wins material by setting up a series of Knight forks with **1 Qxg8!**
Rxg8 2 Nf6+ Ke7 3 Nxg8+ Ke8 4 Nf6+ Ke7 5 Nxd7.

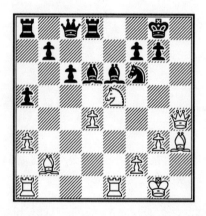

Diagram 88. Taimanov versus Kuzminikh,
Leningrad, 1950. What is White's best move?

Answer: White uses a variety of themes to force the win of material, which
includes an overworked defender (Black's "f" Pawn), a fork and removing the guard.
White played **1 Ng6!** (threatening 2 Qh8++) **Nh7** (not 1...fxg6 because of 2 Bxe6+,
which forks the King and Queen) **2 Rxe6! fxe6 3 Qxd8+ Nf8** (Black cannot play
3...Qxd8 because of 4 Bxe6++) **4 Qxd6.**

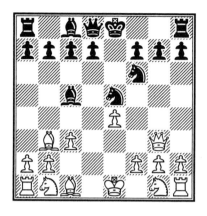

Diagram 89. Amateur versus Leonhardt, Leipzig, 1903. What is Black's best move?

Answer: **1...Bxf2+!** 2 Qxf2 (or if 2 Kxf2 then 2...Nxe4+) **Nd3+ 3 Ke2 Nxf2.**

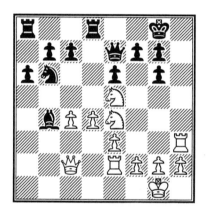

Diagram 90. What is White's best move?

Answer: White wins Black's Queen after **1 Ng5!**. White's threats include 2 Nxg6 fxg6 3 Qxg6 and 2 Ngxf7 threatening 3 Rh8++, which forces Black to give up his Queen with 2...Qxf7 3 Nxf7. After **1 Ng5!** if **1...Qxg5** (or if 1...f5, then 2 Rh8+ Kxh8 3 Nxg6+ Kg8 4 Nxe7+) **2 Rh8+ Kxh8 3 Nxf7+ Kg8 4 Nxg5.**

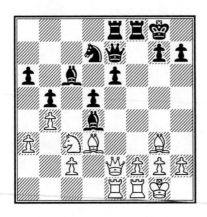

Diagram 91. Snyder versus Hyldkrog, Correspondence, 1977–79. What is White's best move?

Answer: White won a Pawn with **1 Bxh7+ Kxh7 2 Qd3+ Kg8 3 Qxd4**.

We will examine a variety of positions where the use of a *"pin"* is the main theme.

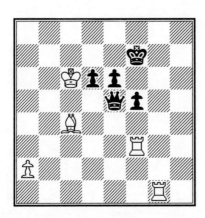

Diagram 92. What is White's best move?

Answer: White simplifies and obtains an easily won endgame with **1 Rxf5+! Qxf5 2 Rf1** followed by capturing Black's Queen and advancing the "a" Pawn.

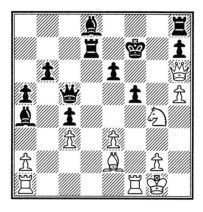

Diagram 93. What is White's best move?

Answer: **1 Bxc4!**. White wins a Pawn while threatening and pinning Black's "e" Pawn. If Black defends the "e" Pawn with **1...Rd6** (not 1...Qxc4?? because of 2 Ne5+) White continues with **2 Rxf5+ Qxf5 3 Rf1 Qxf1+ 4 Bxf1** and White's threats of 5 Qf4+ and 5 Ne5+ are overwhelming.

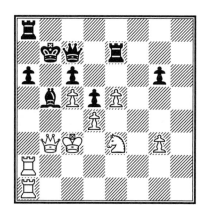

Diagram 94. What is White's best move?

Answer: **1 Nxd5! cxd5 2 Qxb5+ axb5 3 Rxa8** (Black cannot save his Queen) **3...Kc6 4 R1a6+ Kb7** (if 4...Kd7 then 5 Rd6+! Qxd6 6 cxd6) 5 **R8a7+ Kc8 6 Rxc7+ Rxc7 7 Rxg6** winning easily.

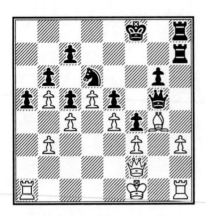

Diagram 95. Popovsky versus Khavin, Lodz, 1940. What is Black's best move?

Answer: Black takes advantage of the pin on White's "h" Pawn with **1…Nxe4! 2 fxe4 Qxg4 3 Qg2** (if 3 hxg4 then 3…Rxh1+ 4 Qg1 Rxg1+ 5 Kxg1 and Black will win easily in the endgame by winning a second Pawn with either 5…Rh3 or 5…Rh4) **Qxg2+ 4 Kxg2 g5** threatening 5…g4 and winning a second Pawn.

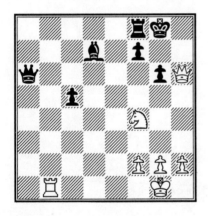

Diagram 96. What is White's best move?

Answer: **1 Nh5** threatening mate on "g7." Black must lose his Queen after **1…gxh5 2 Qxa6.**

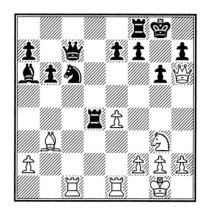

Diagram 97. Carrouse versus Khasoff, Correspondence, 1948. What is White's best move?

Answer: White wins Black's Knight with **1 Rxc6!**. If Black recaptures with **1...Qxc6** then White plays **2 Nh5** and Black must lose his Queen to prevent mate on "g7".

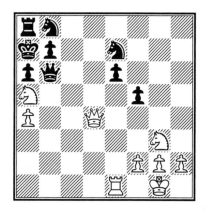

Diagram 98. What is White's best move?

Answer: White wins Black's Queen with **1 Rb1!**. Black cannot play 1...Qxd4 because of 2 Rxb7++.

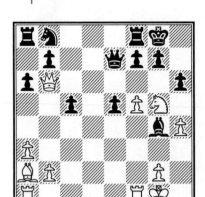

Diagram 99. What is White's best move?

Answer: 1 Qg6! (White threatens 2 Qh7++) **hxg5** (if 1...Bxf5 2 Rxf5 hxg5 3 Raf1! with the plan of 4 Rxf7) **2 f6!** (White threatens both 3 Qxg7++ and 3 fxe7) **Qxf6 3 Rxf6**.

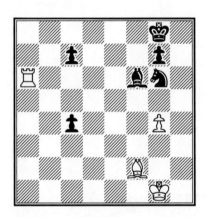

Diagram 100. What is White's best move?

Answer: White wins a piece with **1 g5 Bxg5 2 Rxg6**.

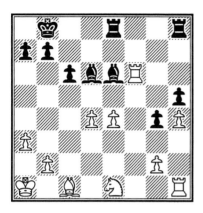

Diagram 101. What is White's best move?

Answer: White wins a Bishop after **1 d5 cxd5 2 exd5 Bxd5 3 Rxd6**.

We will examine a variety of positions where the use of a *"skewer"* (also known as an *"X-ray attack"*) is the main theme.

Diagram 102. What is White's best move?

Answer: **1 Qd1+** followed by **2 Qxd6**.

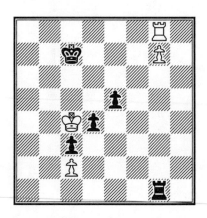

Diagram 103. What is White's best move?

Answer: **1 Ra8!** (threatening 2 g8=Q) **2 Rxg7 Ra7+** followed by **3 Rxg7**.

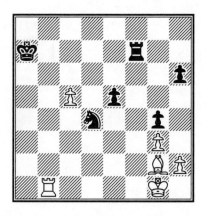

Diagram 104. What is White's best move?

Answer: **1 Ra1+ Kb8 2 Ra8+ Kc7 3 Ra7+** followed by **4 Rxf7**.

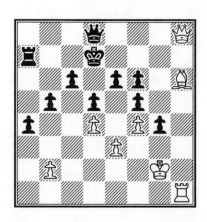

Diagram 105. What is White's best move?

Answer: **1 Qh7+ Qe7 2 Bf8 Qxh7 3 Rxh7+ Ke8 4 Rxa7**.

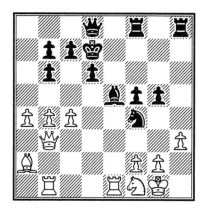

Diagram 106. What is White's best move?

Answer: White wins material with **1 Rxe5 dxe5 2 Rd1+ Kc8 3 Rxd8+**.

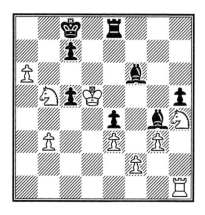

Diagram 107. What is Black's best move?

Answer: **1...Re5+ 2 Kc4** (if 2 Kc6?? then 2...Bd7++) **Be2+ 3 Kc3 Bxb5**.

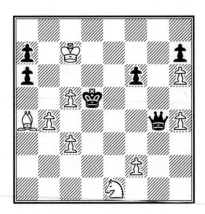

Diagram 108. What is White's best move?

Answer: White uses a skewer or fork as the main winning idea after **1 Ng2!** (White's immediate threat is the fork with 2 Ne3+) **Ke5** (if 1...Qxg2 then 2 Bc6+ followed by 3 Bxg2, or if 1...Ke4 2 f3+ Kxf3 3 Bd1+ followed by 4 Bxg4) **2 f4+ Ke4** (if 2...Ke6 then 3 Bd7+ followed by 4 Bxg4) **3 Bc2+ Kf3 4 Bd1+** followed by **5 Bxg4**.

We will examine a variety of positions where the use of a *"discovered attack"* is the main theme.

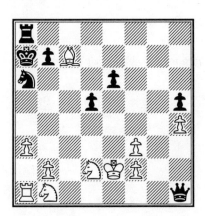

Diagram 109. What is White's best move?

Answer: **1 Nc3!** (White now attacks Black's Queen and threatens 2 Nb5++) **Nxc7** **2 Rxh1**.

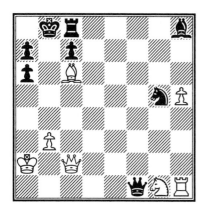

Diagram 110. Fleischer versus Amateur, Switzerland, 1938. What is White's best move?

Answer: Black is threatening 1...Qa1++. Therefore, White uses two discovered attacks on Black's Queen with a Rook sacrifice to set up mate threats of his own with **1 Nf3 Qxh1 2 Ne5** attacking Black's Queen and threatening 3 Nd7++. Black must now lose his Queen to prevent an immediate mate.

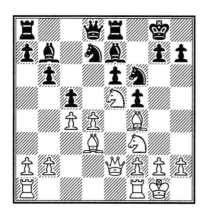

Diagram 111. Alekhine versus Feldt, Tarnopol, 1916. What is White's best move?

Answer: White played **1 Nf7!** (stronger than 1 Nc6 Bxc6 2 Qxe6+ Kh8 3 Qxc6, which would also have won for White) **Kxf7?**. Black would have held out longer but would still have been losing after 1...Qc8 2 Qxe6 (threatening 3 Nh6+ Kh8 4 Qg8+! followed by 5 Nf7++) Ne5 3 Nh6+ Kh8 4 Qxe5 gxh6 5 Bxf5. After **1...Kxf7?** White played **2 Qxe6+! Kg6** (if 2...Kxe6 then 3 Ng5++, or if 2...Kf8 then 3 Ng5) **3 g4** and Black cannot prevent mate on the next move due to the threats of 4 Bxf5++ and 4 Nh4++.

Diagram 112. Canal versus Amateur, Simultaneous Exhibition, Budapest, 1934. What is White's best move?

Answer: The game concluded **1 axb4! Qxa1+ 2 Kd2 Qxh1 3 Qxc6+! bxc6 4 Ba6++**.

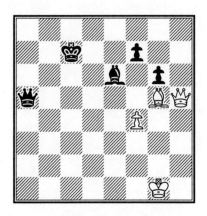

Diagram 113. What is White's best move?

Answer: 1 Bd8+ Kxd8 2 Qxa5+.

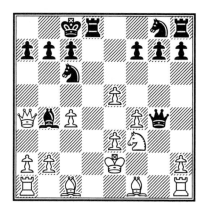

Diagram 114. Blasej versus Mikulka, Correspondence, 1930. What is Black's best move?

Answer: **1...Nxe5!** (threatening 2...Qxf3++) **2 fxe5** (not 2 Qxb4? because of 2...Qxf3+ 3 Ke1 Rd1++) **Qxc4+ 3 Kf2 Be1+ 4 Kxe1 Qxa4**.

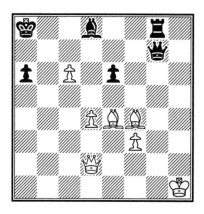

Diagram 115. What is White's best move?

Answer: 1 c7+ Ka7 2 c8=N++!.

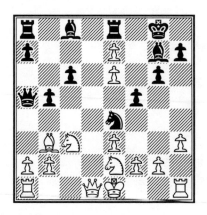

Diagram 116. Gereben versus Szollosy, Budapest, 1948. What is White's best move?

Answer: White played **1 Qd8!** (threatening Black's unprotected Queen and Rook) **Rxd8 2 exd8=Q+ Qxd8 3 e7+ Be6 4 Bxe6+ Kh8 5 exd8=Q+**.

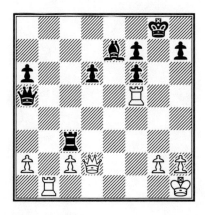

Diagram 117. Maric versus Gligoric, Belgrade, 1962. What is Black's best move?

Answer: After **1...Rb3!** White resigned because all of his major pieces are under attack and Black has a back-rank mate threat as well. If White tries getting his Queen out of attack and defending his Rook on "b1" with 2 Qd1, then Black will be a piece and Pawn ahead after 2...Rxb1 3 Qxb1 Qxf5.

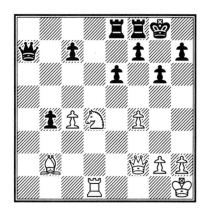

Diagram 118. What is White's best move?

Answer: White uses a discovered attack to win Black's Queen with **1 Nf5! exf5** (not 1...Qxf2? because of 2 Nh6++, or if 1...gxf5? then 2 Qg3++) **2 Qxa7.**

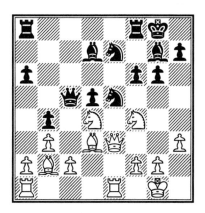

Diagram 119. Snyder versus Dean, San Diego, 1975. What is White's best move?

Answer: White won a couple of Pawns using a discovered attack on Black's Queen after **1 Nf5! Qxe3 2 Nxe7 + Kf7 3 Rxe3 Kxe7 4 Nxd5+** forking the King and the "b" Pawn.

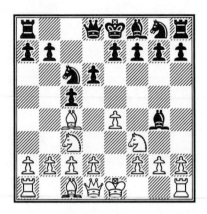

Diagram 120. What is White's best move?

Answer: 1 Bxf7+ Kxf7 2 Ng5+ Ke8 3 Qxg4.

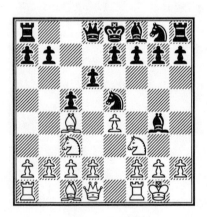

Diagram 121. What is White's best move?

Answer: 1 Nxe5! dxe5 (if 1...Bxd1? then 2 Bxf7++) 2 Qxg4.

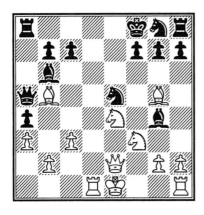

Diagram 122. What is White's best move?

Answer: 1 Nxe5! Bxe2 2 Nd7+ Ke8 3 Nb8+! (The key move, which blocks Black's Rook along the 8th rank at the right moment) **c6** (if 3...Qxb5 then 4 Rd8++ —the reason for White's 3rd move is now apparent) **4 Nd6+ Kf8 5 Nd7++.**

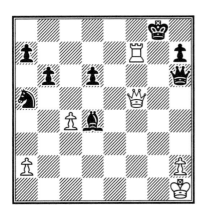

Diagram 123. What is White's best move?

Answer: 1 Qd5!. White will have a killer discovered check when he moves his Rook—there is no place to hide! If 1...Kh8 then 2 Qa8+ Qf8 3 Qxf8++.

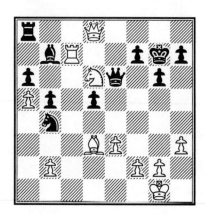

Diagram 124. What is White's best move?

Answer: 1 Nxf7! Rxd8 2 Nxd8+ Kf6 3 Nxe6 Kxe6 (if 3...Nxd3 then 4 Nd4! and Black's Bishop is trapped) **4 Bxb5!** winning easily.

We will now examine some positions with mixed or miscellaneous themes.

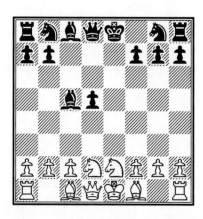

Diagram 125. What is Black's best move?

Answer: Black takes advantage of White's weak "f2" square and threatens mate with **1...Qb6!**. If 2 Nf3?, then 2...Bxf2+ 3 Kd2 Qe3++. White has nothing better to do than to give up a Knight to prevent mate with 2 Nd4 Bxd4 3 Qf3.

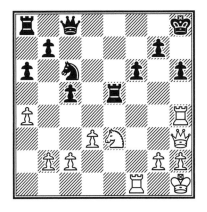

Diagram 126. Snyder versus Oakes, Simultaneous Exhibition, Anaheim, 1978. What is White's best move?

Answer: Black's King was exposed to a deadly attack with **1 Rxh6+! gxh6** (Black would lose his Queen after 1...Kg8 2 Rh8+ Kf7 3 Rxc8) **2 Qxh6+ Kg8 3 Qg6+ Kf8** (if 3...Kh8 then 4 Rf4 with the idea of 5 Rh4+) **4 Rxf6+ Ke7 5 Rf7+ Kd8 6 Qd6+ Ke8 7 Rf8++.**

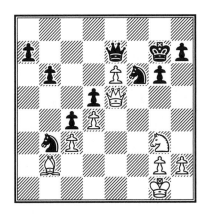

Diagram 127. Botvinnik versus Capablanca, AVRO, 1938. What is White's best move?

Answer: White began a deep combination with **1 Ba3!**, which continued **1...Qxa3** (if 1...Qe8 then 2 Qc7+ Kg8 3 Be7 Kg7 4 Bd8+ or if 3...Ng4 then 4 Qd7) **2 Nh5+ gxh5** (if 2...Kh6 then 3 Nxf6 Qc1+ 4 Kf2 Qd2+ 5 Kg3 Qxc3+ 6 Kh4 Qxd4+ 7 Ng4+) **3 Qg5+ Kf8 4 Qxf6+ Kg8 5 e7** (5 Qf7+ Kh8 6 g3 followed by advancing the Pawn to "e7" would have been more accurate) **Qc1+ 6 Kf2 Qc2+ 7 Kg3 Qd3+ 8 Kh4 Qe4+ 9 Kxh5 Qe2+ 10 Kh4 Qe4+ 11 g4** (if 11 Kh3 then 11...h5) **Qe1+ 12 Kh5** and Black has run out of checks.

The ability to find good defensive resources can be every bit as important as knowing how to attack. In the next position Black misses an opportunity to limit White's advantage.

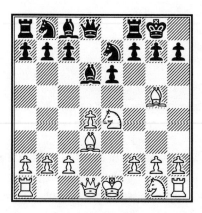

Diagram 128. Blom versus Jensen, Denmark, 1934. What is White's best move?

Answer: 1 Nf6+! gxf6 (refusing the sacrifice with 1...Kh8 loses quickly after 2 Qh5 h6 3 Bxh6) **2 Bxf6 Qd7?** (at this point Black misses a great defensive resource with 2...Bb4+! 3 Kf1! Qd5! 4 c4 Qa5 5 a3 Ng6 6 axb4 Qxb4 7 h4 Nd7 and, though White still has an attack, Black would have avoided immediate disaster) **3 Bxh7+ Kxh7 4 Qh5+ Kg8 5 Qh8++.**

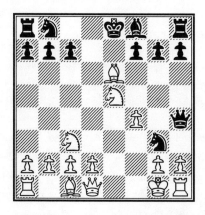

Diagram 129. Efimov versus Bronstein, Kiev, 1938. What is Black's best move?

Answer: 1...Bc5+ 2 d4 Bxd4+ 3 Qxd4 Ne2+ and White has a choice of getting checkmated with 4 Nxe2 Qe1++ or losing his Queen with 4 Kf1 Nxd4.

Diagram 130. Troitsky, 1906. What is White's best move?

Answer: **1 Ng2!** (White threatens 2 Nxh4, which would win easily) **hxg3+ 2 Kg1 h5 3 Kh1 h4 4 Nf4++**.

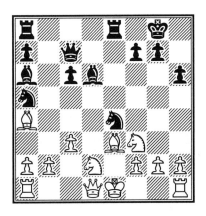

Diagram 131. Balk versus Barnes, New Zealand, 1926. What is Black's best move?

Answer: The game continued **1...Nxc3! 2 bxc3 Rxe3+! 3 fxe3 Bg3+ 4 hxg3 Qxg3++**.

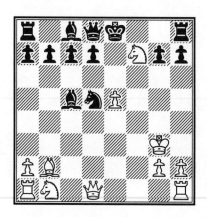

Diagram 132. Hoffman versus Petroff, Warsaw, 1844. What is Black's best move?

Answer: The game continued **1...0-0! 2 Nxd8 Bf2+ 3 Kh3 d6+ 4 e6 Nf4+ 5 Kg4 Nxe6 6 Nxe6 Bxe6+ 7 Kg5 Rf5+ 8 Kg4 h5+ 9 Kh3 Rf3++**.

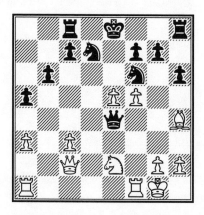

Diagram 133. Lilienthal versus Capablanca, Hastings, 1934–35. What is White's best move?

Answer: White won with a deep Queen sacrifice after **1 exf6! Qxc2 2 fxg7 Rg8 3 Nd4** (this attacks Black's Queen while opening up the "e" file for use against Black's King) **Qe4 4 Rae1 Nc5 5 Rxe4+ Nxe4 6 Re1 Rxg7 7 Rxe4+**.

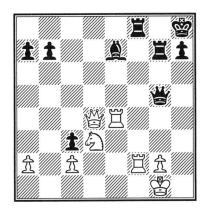

Diagram 134. Spassky versus Fischer, Mar del Plata, 1960. What is White's best move?

Answer: White attacks Black's Queen with the idea of driving her away from the protection of the Bishop on "e7" with **1 Re5**. The game continued **1...Rd8** (if 1...Bf6 then 2 Qd6 threatening 3 Rxg5 and 3 Qxf8+) **2 Qe4 Qh4 3 Rf4** and Black must lose his Bishop on "e7".

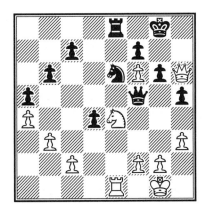

Diagram 135. What is White's best move?

Answer: **1 Nd6! cxd6** (Black's game would be hopelessly lost after 1...Qxf6 2 Nxe8) **2 Rxe6!** and Black cannot defend against the threats of 3 Qg7++ and 3 Rxe8++.

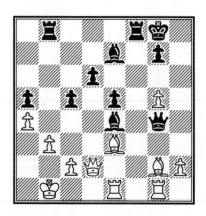

Diagram 136. What is White's best move?

Answer: White wins a Bishop after **1 Qd5+! Bxd5 2 Bxd5+ Kh7 3 Rxg4**.

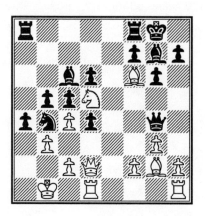

Diagram 137. What is White's best move?

Answer: **1 Qh6!**. Black cannot prevent mate. White immediately threatens 2 Qxg7++. **If 1...Bxh6** then **2 Ne7++. Or if 1...Bxf6** then **2 Nxf6+ Kh8 3 Qxh7++.**

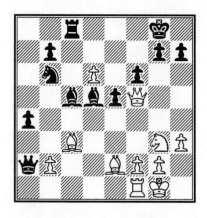

Diagram 138. What is White's best move?

Answer: **1 Qxc8+! Nxc8 2 d7 Ne7 3 d8=Q+.**

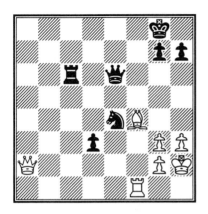

Diagram 139. What is White's best move?

Answer: **1 Bd6!**. White threatens both 2 Rf8++ and 2 Qxe6+. If 1...Rxd6 then 2 Qa8+ leads to mate.

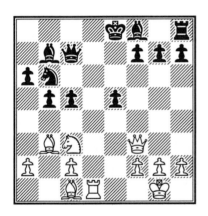

Diagram 140. What is White's best move?

Answer: **1 Bxf7+ Qxf7** (if 1...Ke7 then 2 Bg5++) **2 Rd8+ Kxd8** (if 2...Ke7 then 3 Bg5+) **3 Qxf7**.

Studying Endgames

When it comes to study and preparation, the endgame is the most neglected part of the game. I have students who have labored for hours in a tournament game to achieve a winning position, only to throw everything away because they didn't know a basic endgame idea.

The good news is that if you learn the most important basic endgame ideas they will go a long way in helping you in almost every endgame position you reach. Be sure you thoroughly understand the most basic endgames before studying more complicated examples. Often, finding the right moves in a more complex endgame becomes a matter of calculation to reach a basic endgame. Knowing the result and the procedure of the basic endgame then gives you a jump off point (you don't need to calculate any further). However, some endgames can be extremely complicated. In such cases knowing the basics will certainly help, but there may be no substitute for long hard thought.

My *Chess for Juniors* book already covered the most basic checkmates (King and Queen versus King, King and Rook versus King) and the most basic King and Pawn endings, which include the idea of the opposition. Therefore, in this book we will continue where *Chess for Juniors* left off, with some examples of the most important basic endgames. It will be assumed you know the material covered in *Chess for Juniors*. For a comprehensive one-volume book on the endgame I recommend *Basic Chess Endings* by Reuben Fine, algebraic edition (New York: Random House, 2003).

We will begin by looking at some important positions in King and Pawn endings. In the first diagram White needs to achieve the "basic winning position" with the King on the 6th rank in front of the Pawn on the 5th rank.

Diagram 141. White to move and win.

Answer: 1 Kc7. This is the only move that will win (if 1 b6+? Ka8 results in a draw). **1...Ka8 2 Kb6** (White has now achieved the "basic winning position") **Kb8 3 Ka6** (if 3 Kc6 then we are back to the starting position after 3...Ka7) **Ka8 4 b6 Kb8 5 b7** (an easy rule to remember in the basic King and Pawn versus King ending is *when the King is supporting the advance of the Pawn, if the Pawn reaches the 7th rank with check it is a draw, without check it is a win*) **Kc7 6 Ka7** and the Pawn Queens.

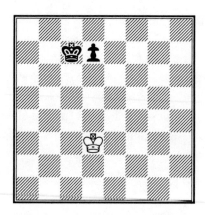

Diagram 142. White to move and draw.

Answer: White uses the *"distant opposition"* to achieve a draw with **1 Kc3!**. Any other move would allow Black to obtain the opposition and win—for example: if 1 Ke4 Kc6 2 Kd4 Kd6 3 Ke4 Kc5) **Kc6** (if 1...Kd6 then 2 Kd4, or if 1...Kb6 then either 2 Kb4 or 2 Kd4 is a draw) **2 Kc4** with a basic draw as covered in my book *Chess for Juniors.* For example if 2...Kd6 White maintains the opposition with 3 Kd4 Ke6 4 Ke4.

Diagram 143. White to move and win.

Answer: White has a case of what I call *"forever protecting Pawns."* White's King, wherever he may be, has all the time he needs to head toward the Pawns to support them to obtain a Queen. **1 Ke5 Kh8 2 Ke6** (2 Kf6?? would be stalemate!) **Kg7 3 h8=Q+ Kxh8 4 Kf6** (4 Kf7?? would be stalemate!) **Kg8 5 g7 Kh7 6 Kf7** and the Pawn Queens.

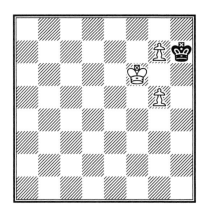

Diagram 144. White to move and win/Black to move and draw.

Answer: If it was Black's turn to move this position would be a draw after **1...Kg8**.

With White to move the only winning method is to sacrifice the Pawn on "g7" to obtain the basic winning position: **1 g8=Q+ Kxg8 2 Kg6 Kh8 3 Kf7** and the Pawn goes marching on!

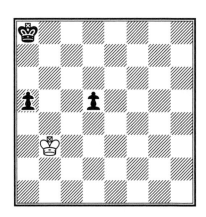

Diagarm 145. White to move and draw/Black to move and win.

Answer: If it was Black's turn to move Black would win with **1...Kb7 2 Kc3 Kc6 3 Kd4 a4** (3...Kd6 would also do the job) **4 Kc3 Kc5 5 Kd3 a3 6 Kc3 a2 7 Kb2 Kd4 8 Kxa2 Ke3**.

With White to move the game is a draw after **1 Ka4 d4** (we reach a basic drawn position after 1...Kb7 2 Kxa5 Kc6 3 Kb4 Kd6 4 Kc3 Ke5 5 Kd3) **2 Kb3 Kb7 3 Kc4 Kc6 4 Kxd4 Kb5 5 Kc3** with a basic drawn position.

Diagram 146. White to move and win.

Answer: The Pawns help aid each other in their advance and give White's King the time he needs to come to their aid. **1 c4 Ka5 2 Kg2** (2 c5?? would be a draw after 2...Kb5 followed by capturing "c" Pawn) **Kb6** (Black threatens to win White's "c" Pawn with 3...Kc5 followed by 4...Kxc4) **3 a4 Kc5 4 a5 Kc6 5 Kf3 Kb7 6 c5 Ka6 7 c6 Ka7 8 Ke4 Ka6 9 Kd5 Ka7 10 Kd6** (White avoids falling into the trap by playing 10 c7?? Kb7 11 Kd6 Kc8 resulting in a draw—sometimes patience is required in the endgame!) **Kb8 11 Kd7** (once again advancing the "c" prematurely with 11 c7+ Kc8 would result in a draw) **Ka8** (Black has one more trap up his sleeve, making the best out of a lost position) **12 c7 Ka7 13 Kc6!** (this forces a mate in four moves—Black was hoping that White would prematurely Queen his Pawn with 13 c8=Q resulting in stalemate) **Ka6 14 c8=Q+ Kxa5 15 Qg4! Ka6 16 Qa4++.**

Diagram 147. White to move and win.

Answer: If White steams forward and directly attacks Black's Pawn while defending his own with 1 Kd5?? then Black plays 1...Kf4 placing White in zugzwang and Black wins. Therefore, White uses a simple form of what is called *"triangulation"* and plays **1 Kd6!**. Black's King now must defend his Pawn with **1...Kf4** allowing White to put him in zugzwang with **2 Kd5**. Black's King must now abandon the protection of his Pawn, which falls after **2...Kg5 3 Kxe5**.

Diagram 148. White to move and win/Black to move and win.

Answer: Whoever has the move will Queen first and attack the Queening square of the other Pawn. This is a common situation involving "a" and "h" Pawns on opposite sides of the board. White to move would win with **1 a5 h4 2 a6 h3 3 a7 h2 4 a8=Q**.

Diagram 149. White to move and win.

Answer: White has his choice of two winning methods. **1 b7 Ka7** (if 1...d2 then 2 Kb6 d8=Q 3 a7++) **2 Kc7 Kxa6 3 b8=Q**, or **1 a7+ Ka8 2 Kc7 d2 3 b7+ Kxa7 4 b8=Q+ Ka6 5 Qb6++**.

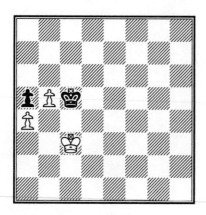

Diagram 150. White to move and win.

Answer: White uses an elaborate maneuver to outflank Black's King and occupy the "c5" square at the right time. **1 Kd3 Kd5 2 Ke3 Ke5 3 Kf3 Kd5** (the Black King cannot continue to oppose White's King with 3...Kf5 because of 4 b6 and the Pawn Queens) **4 Kf4 Kd6 5 Ke4 Ke6 6 Kd4 Kd6 7 Kc4 Kc7 8 Kd5!** (not 8 Kc5 Kb7 9 b6? as 9...Ka6 draws because 10 Kc6 is stalemate—note that if all of the pieces were one more square to the right stalemate wouldn't occur and this plan would be good) **Kb6** (if 8...Kd7 then 9 b6 does the job) **9 Kd6 Kb7 10 Kc5 Kc7** (if 10...Ka7 then 11 Kc6 Kb8 11 Kb6) **11 b6+ Kb7 11 Kb5** and White wins the pawn at a5. Note that if all of the pieces in the starting position were moved up one square, then it would be a draw because of the stalemating possibilities.

Diagram 151. White to move and win.

Answer: **1 Kc7!** (if 1 Kc6 then 1...a5! 2 Kxb5 axb4 3 axb4 Kb7 results in a draw) **a5** (if 1...Ka8 then 2 Kb6) **2 a4! Ka6** (if 2...bxa4 then 3 b5 a3 4 b6+ Ka6 5 b7 a2 6 b8=Q a8=Q 7 Qb7++, or if 2...axb4 then 3 axb5 b3 4 b6+ Ka6 5 b7 b2 6 b8=Q) **3 Kc6 axb4** (if 3...bxa4 then 4 b5+ Ka7 5 Kc7 and the "b" advances, or if 3...Ka7 then

4 axb5 axb4 5 Kc7 and the "b" Pawn advances) **4 axb5+ Ka5 5 b6** and White's Pawn will Queen first.

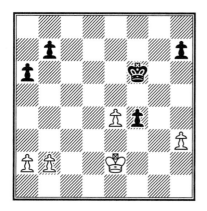

Diagram 152. Schwede versus Sika, Brno, 1929. Black to move and win.

Answer: Even in King and Pawn endings with many Pawns on the board, having an extra tempo (move) can make all the difference. Black runs White out of moves while keeping his extra tempo in reserve to force White into zugzwang. **1...Ke5 2 Kf3 a5!** (without this move, which will keep Black's "b" Pawn as the reserve tempo, it would be Black who would end up in zugzwang: 2...b6? 3 h4! a5 4 a4 h6 5 h5 and Black is in zugzwang and must lose his "f" Pawn) **3 b3** (if 4 a4 then 4...h6! will run White out of Pawn moves) **b5 4 a3** (if 4 a4 then 4...b4 5 h4 h5, or if 4 h4 then 4...b4 5 h5 h6) **b4 5 axb4** (if 5 a4 then 5...h6! 6 h4 h5) **axb4 6 h4 h5.** A key factor in many endgames, where a tempo is important, is keeping a Pawn on the second rank where it has the option of moving one or two squares.

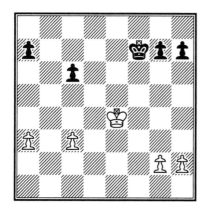

Diagram 153. Opocensky versus Prokop, Prague, 1942. White to move and win.

Answer: White's more active King position prevents Black from being able to advance his "c" Pawn. This will give White's "c" Pawn critical extra tempos. **1 Ke5 Ke7**

(Black must prevent White's King from entering "d6") **2 g4** (White will advance his Pawns on the Kingside to attack Black's Pawns, with the idea of forcing another possible point of penetration for White's King) **Kd7** (If Black played 2...h6 he would have opened the "g6" square for possible penetration by White's King, which might have continued 3 Kf5 Kf7 4 a4 a6 5 a5 Ke7 6 Kg6 Kf8 7 h3 Kg8 8 h4 Kf8 9 Kh7 Kf7 10 g5 hxg5 11 hxg5 g6 12 Kh6 c5 13 c4) **3 g5 Ke7 4 h4 Kd7 5 h5 Ke7 6 a4 a6** (less resistance was offered in the actual game, which continued 6...a5 7 c4 Kd7 8 h6 g6 9 Kf6 Kd6 10 Kg7 and Black resigned because 10...Ke7 11 Kxh7 Kf7 is met by 12 c5) **7 a5 Kd7 8 h6 gxh6 9 gxh6 Ke7 10 c4 Kd7 11 Kf6 Kd6** (if 11...c5 then 12 Ke5 Kc6 13 Ke6 Kc7 14 Kd5) **12 Kg7 Ke7 13 Kxh7 Kf7 14 c5** (as mentioned previously, the critical tempo provided by this Pawn has won the day) **Kf8 15 Kg6 Kg8 16 Kf6** and Black's "c" Pawn will become a yummy snack for White's King.

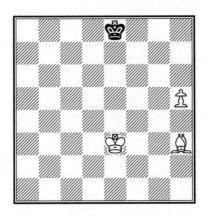

Diagram 154. Troitzky, 1896. White to move and win.

Answer: As a general rule, *"Against a lone King, when one side has only a Bishop and an "a" or "h" Pawn remaining on the board (where the Bishop isn't of the same color as the Queening square of the Pawn) the game is a draw if the enemy King can get to the corner in front of the Pawn."* Therefore, in order to win White cannot allow Black's King to get to "h8". **1 Be6 Ke7** (1...Kf8 would lose quickly after 2 h6 Ke7 3 h7) **2 h6 Kf6 3 Bf5 Kf7 4 Bh7! Kf6 5 Kf4 Kf7 6 Kf5 Kf8 7 Kf6 Ke8 8 Bf5 Kf8** (Black could avoid mate longer by running the other way) **9 h7 Ke8 10 h8=Q++** (or 10 h8=R++!).

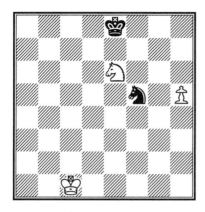

Diagram 155. White to move and win.

Answer: **1 Ng7+ Nxg7** (if 1...Kf7 then 2 Nxf5 Kf6 3 h6 Kg6 and White's King heads to the rescue with 4 Kd2) **2 h6 Kf7 3 h7** and the Pawn Queens.

Diagram 156. White to move and draw.

Answer: The Knight is a natural born blockader of Pawns. As a general rule, *"A lone Pawn that has reached its 7th rank (with the exception of an "a" or "h" Pawn) against a lone King is a draw if the Knight can get in front of the Pawn."* **1 Nb1 Kc2 2 Na3+ Kb3 3 Nb1 Ka2 4 Nc3+** (or 4 Nd2 followed by 5 Kf2 draws) **Kb3 5 Nb1** and Black can make no progress.

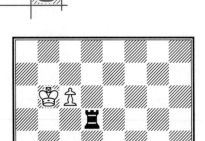

Diagram 157. Saavedra, 1895. White to move and win.

Answer: Here we have an instance where a King and Pawn versus a King and Rook wins. **1 c7 Rd6+ 2 Kb5 Rd5+ 3 Kb4 Rd4+ 4 Kb3** (4 Kc3 Rd1 5 Kc2 also wins in a similar manner to the text) **Rd3+ 5 Kc2 Rd4!** (Black sees a neat way of setting a trap—in practical play you will find that on occasion you can save yourself in a lost position by being resourceful) **6 c8=R!** (the only move that wins and threatens 7 Ra8+—White avoided playing 6 c8=Q?? Rc4+! 7 Qxc4 stalemate) **Ra4 7 Kb3.** White wins Black's Rook because of his threats of 8 Rc1++ and 8 Kxa4.

Diagram 158. White to move and win.

Answer: The idea in this King and Rook versus a King and Pawn ending is to cut the King off from the fifth rank. This will prevent Black's King from advancing to support his Pawn. As a result Black will have the choice of allowing White's King to come to play or advance the Pawn and lose it. **1 Rb5!** (if it was Black to move the game would have been a draw after 1...Kg5) **h3** (other moves allow White's King to come into play) **2 Rb3 h2 3 Rh3** and the Pawn dies.

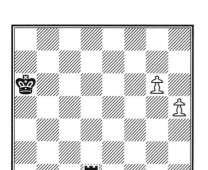

Diagram 159. White to move and win/Black to move and win.

Answer: As a general rule, *"In a Rook versus two connected Pawns ending where the Kings are out of play, the Pawns will win if they are both on the 6th rank, but if one Pawn is on the 5th rank and one on the 6th with the side with the Rook having the move then the Rook will win."* White to move can win with either **1 h6 Rg2** (or if 1...Rh2 then 2 g7 Rg2 3 h7) **2 h7 Rh2 3 g7** and White Queens a Pawn, or **1 g7 Rg2 2 h6 Kb6 3 h7** and White Queens a Pawn.

Black to move would win with **1...Rg2 2 Kb1 Rg5** (bringing the King over to capture the Pawns beginning with 2...Kb6 would also do the job) **3 Kc2 Rxh5 4 g7 Rg5**.

Diagram 160. Inkjov versus Doncev, Varna, 1979. White to move and win.

Answer: Black's connected passed Pawns have already advanced to a point where the Rook cannot prevent their continued advance and White's King is out of range. Therefore, White comes up with a unique resource. **1 Kf6! d3 2 e6 d2 3 Rg7+ Kh6** (if 3...Kh8 then 2 e7 followed by 3 e8=Q++) **4 Rg8** (threatening 5 Rh8++) **Kh7 5 Rh8+ Kxh8 6 e7 d1=Q e8=Q+ 7 Kh7 Qf7+ 8 Kh8 Qg7++**.

It isn't uncommon for both players to be left with just one Pawn where a critical race takes place to Queen their Pawns.

As a general rule, *"In a King and Queen against a King and Pawn ending where the Pawn has reached the 7th rank supported by the King, the side with the Queen will win if the Pawn is a "b," "d," "e," or "g" Pawn and will draw if the Pawn is an "a," "c," "f," or "h" Pawn"(assuming that the side with the Queen has the King too far from the action)."*

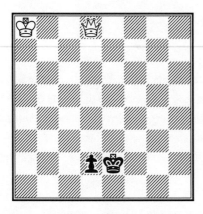

Diagram 161. White to move and win.

Answer: The winning idea is to force Black to move his King in front of his Pawn to give White time to move his King in to assist. This pattern is also used to win against a "b," "e," or "g" Pawn. **1 Qe7+ Kf2 2 Qf6+ Ke2 3 Qe5+ Kf2 4 Qd4+ Ke2 5 Qe4+ Kf2 6 Qd3!** (the key winning idea, which will soon force Black's King to move in front of his Pawn) **Ke1 7 Qe3+ Kd1 8 Kb7 Kc2 9 Qe2 Kc1 10 Qc4+ Kb2 11 Qd3 Kc1 12 Qc3+ Kd1 13 Kc6 Ke2 14 Qc2 Ke1 15 Qe4+ Kf2 16 Qd3 Ke1 17 Qe3+ Kd1 18 Kd5 Kc2 19 Qe2 Kc1 20 Qc4+ Kb2 21 Qd3 Kc1 22 Qc3+ Kd1 23 Kd4 Ke2 24 Qe3+ Kd1 25 Kc3 Kc1 26 Qxd2+ Kb1 27 Qb2++.**

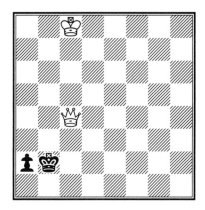

Diagram 162. White to move and draw.

Answer: The winning pattern used in the previous position against a center Pawn only results in a draw against an "a" or "h" Pawn. **1 Qb4+ Kc2 2 Qa3 Kb1 3 Qb3+ Ka1!**. White cannot move his King to assist with **4 Kc7** because this would result in stalemate. White is unable to make progress.

Diagram 163. White to move and draw.

Answer: Black also uses a stalemate theme to draw with an "f" or "c" Pawn. **1 Qg4+ Kh2 2 Qf3 Kg1 3 Qg3+ Kh1!**. White cannot capture Black's Pawn with **4 Qxf2** because this would result in stalemate. White is unable to make any progress.

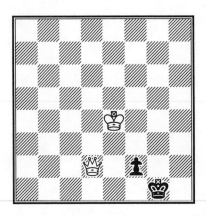

Diagram 164. White to move and win. Snyder versus Amateur, Downey, 1971.

Answer: White's King is just within range to set up a neat mate! **1 Kf3! f1=Q+ 2 Kg3.** My opponent resigned because he cannot prevent mate.

Some critical and instructive positions come about when we have a King, Rook, and Pawn against a King and Rook. In the following position we have a fine illustration of *"Philidor's Position,"* a well-known method of obtaining a draw.

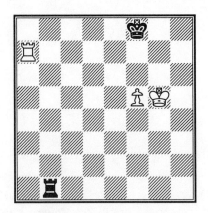

Diagram 165. Black to move and draw.

Answer: The famous 18th-century player André Philidor pointed out that in the above position an easy draw can be achieved by cutting off White's King on Black's third rank by playing **1...Rb6!**. The plan is to meet **2 f6** with **2...Rb1!**. Black can then harass White's King by constant checks with the Rook. However, the game is also drawn after **1...Rf1 2 Kf6 Kg8** (not 2...Ke8?? because White wins after 3 Ra8+ Kd7 4 Rf8! Rh1 5 Kg7 Rg1+ 6 Kf7 Rf1 7 f6 Rg1 8 Rg8 Rf1 9 Kg7 and now if 9...Ke6 then 10 Re8+ Kf5 11 f7 Rg1+ 12 Kf8 Kf6 13 Ra8 Rb1 14 Ra6+ Kf5 15 Kg8 Rg1+ 16 Kh7 Rh1+ 17 Rh6, or if 9...Rg1+ then 10 Kf8 Ra1 11 f7 Ke6 12 Rg3 Rf1 13 Kg8) **3 Ra8+**

Kh7 4 Ke6 (if 4 Rf8 then 4...Ra1 prevents White from making any progress) **Kg7 5 Ra7+ Kf8** and White cannot make progress.

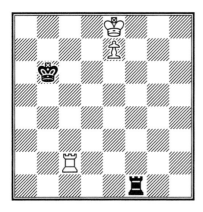

Diagram 166. White to move and win.

Answer: Here we have the famous *"Lucena Position"*. White has more than one method to win. Maneuvering White's Rook to "f8" is most simple. **1 Rh2 Kc7 2 Rh8 Rf2** (if 2...Kd6 then 3 Kd8 Ra1 4 Rh6+ followed by 5 e8=Q) **3 Rf8 Re2 4 Kf7** (This move is given for instructive purposes—however, White also has other winning moves such as 4 Rf1) **Rf2+ 5 Kg6 Rg2+ 6 Kf5 Rf2+ 7 Kg4 Rg2+ 8 Kf3**. Another instructive winning method, referred to as *"building a bridge,"* is **1 Rc4 Rf2 2 Kd7 Rd2+ 3 Ke6 Re2+ 4 Kd6 Rd2+ 5 Ke5 Re2+ 6 Re4**.

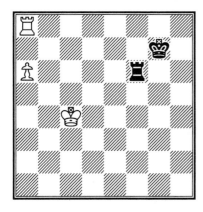

Diagram 167. Vancura, 1924. White to move and draw.

Answer: White's King would like to be able to defend his Pawn, which would free his Rook. However, because Black's Rook can harass the King with checks and/or keep White's Pawn under attack White will not be able to make progress. **1 Kb5** (White now threatens to win with 2 Rc8) **Rf5+ 2 Kc6 Rf6+ 3 Kd5 Rb6 4 Ke5 Rc6 5 a7** (if

5 Ra7+ then 5...Kg8 or 5...Kg6) **Ra6 6 Kd5 Kh7** (not 6...Kf7?? because of 7 Rh8!
Rxa7 8 Rh7+) **7 Kc5 Kg7 8 Kb5 Ra1 9 Kb6 Rb1+**. Black keeps on checking until
the King leaves the area of the Pawn at which time Black would bring his Rook back
to "a1" to attack the Pawn.

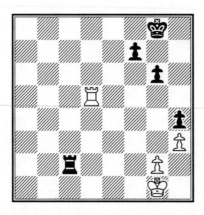

Diagram 168. Levenfish versus Cohn, Carlsbad,
1911. White to move and draw.

Answer: In most cases where all of the Pawns and Kings are on the same side of
the board with one side having an extra Pawn the game should be a draw. However,
there are some exceptions and often such endgames are misplayed. **1 Rd4 g5 2 Rg4
f6 3 g3! hxg3 4 h4! Rc3** (if 4...Rc5 then White can achieve a basic drawn position
with either 5 Rxg3 Kf7 6 hxg5 or 5 hxg5 fxg5 6 Rxg3) **5 hxg5 f5 6 Rf4** with a basic
drawn position.

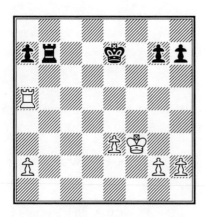

Diagram 169. Rubenstein versus Lasker, St.
Petersburg, 1909. White to move and win.

Answer: 1 Ra6!. White restricts the movement of Black's King so that he cannot
advance beyond his second rank. White will also keep Black's Rook tied down to the
defense of his "a" Pawn. **1...Kf8.** Black has nothing better to do than to wait for White

to come and get him. Black doesn't want to move any of his Kingside Pawns as this would weaken them and give White further opportunities for penetration. **2 e4** (White cautiously advances his passed Pawn) **Rc7 3 h4**. White's plan is twofold. First, he wants to remove his Kingside Pawns from his second rank, because when White advances his King he does not want to give Black an opportunity to attack his Pawns with Rc2. Second, White will advance his Kingside Pawns to eventually force Black to weaken his Kingside Pawns. This will give White more opportunities to penetrate on the Kingside. **3...Kf7 4 g4 Kf8 5 Kf4** (White activates his King) **Ke7 6 h5**. White continues with his plan of advancing his Pawns on the Kingside to eventually force Black to weaken his Pawns. Note that White doesn't just barrel forward with his passed "e" Pawn. White first takes the time to improve his position. The "e" Pawn will eventually have its day. **6...h6** (Black didn't want to allow White to advance his Pawn to "g5" unopposed so he decided to draw the line at this point) **7 Kf5** (White posts his King so that he can support the further advance of his "e" Pawn and has opportunities to penetrate to "g6") **Kf7 8 e5 Rb7 9 Rd6**. White's Rook now has the potential of attacking on the seventh or eighth ranks. The immediate threat is 10 Rd7+! Rxd7 11 e6+ Ke8 12 exd7+ Kxd7 13 Kg6 followed by 14 Kxg7. **9...Kf8** (if 9...Re7 then 10 Rd7!) **10 Rc6**. This was the text move played in the game. However, in the generally excellent book *Rook Endings* by Levenfish and Smyslov, they wrongly claim in their analysis that 10 Rd8+ would be falling for a trap after 10...Kf7 11 e6+ Ke7 12 Rg8 Rb5+ 13 Kg6 Rg5+ 14 Kh7 Rxg4 15 Rxg7+ Rxg7+ 16 Kxg7 Kxe6 17 Kxh6 Kf6 with a drawn ending. The problem with all of this analysis is that they overlooked 12 Rd7+! Rxd7 13 exd7 Kxd7 14 Kg6 winning easily for White. Therefore, 10 Rd8+ was a reasonable alternative to the text move. **10...Kf7 11 a3**. Black is in zugzwang and resigned here. Some possible continuations may have been 11...Ke7 12 Kg6 Kd7 (if 12...Kf8 then 13 Rc8+ Ke7 14 Kxg7) 13 Rd6+ Ke8 14 Re6+ (or 14 e6 also wins easily) Kf8 15 Rc6 Rb8 16 Rc7 Rb6+ 17 Kh7, or 11...Re7 then 12 e6+ Kg8 13 Kg6 Re8 14 e7!, and finally 11...a5 12 Ra6 (or 12 e6+ followed by 13 Kg6 wins) Rb5 13 Ra7+ Kf8 14 a4 Rc5 15 Ke6 Rc6+ 16 Kd5 Rb6 17 Rxa5.

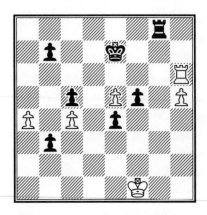

Diagram 170. Street versus Snyder, Santa Monica, 1974. What is Black's best move?

Answer: If it was White's turn to move he would play 1 Rb6 attacking both of Black's "b" Pawns. Therefore, Black played **1...b5!** preventing White's Rook from attacking Black's passed Pawn on "b3" from behind. White resigned. If 2 Rb6 b4 3 Rd6 Rd8.

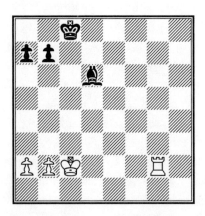

Diagram 171. Reuben Fine, 1941. White to move and win.

Answer: The superiority of the Rook versus a Bishop is clearly shown. The Bishop cannot cover half the squares on the board. White will exploit this weakness by marching his King to "d5" where he can penetrate even further and provoke Black to weaken his Pawns. **1 Kc3 Kc7 2 Kc4 a6.** Here 2...Kc6 only temporarily halts the advance of White's King. After 3 Rg6 b5+ (3...a6 would be similar to the main line after 4 Kd4 Kc7 5 Kd5, and if 4...a5 then 5 Rf6 a4 6 a3 Kc7 7 Kd5) 4 Kd4 Kc7 5 Kd5 Bf8 6 Rf6 Be7 (if 6...Bb4 then 7 a3 Bd2 8 Kc5 wins easily) 7 Rf7 Kd8 (stronger than Fine's 7...Kd7, which allows White to win the upcoming King and Pawn ending faster by playing 8 b4! Ke8 9 Rxe7+ Kxe7 10 Kc6) 8 Rxe7 Kxe7 9 Kc5 Kd7 10 Kxb5 Kc7 11 Ka6 Kb8 12 b4 Ka8 13 b5 Kb8 14 a3! (it is important to have the right tempo when

White's Pawns reach a5 and b6—if White had played 14 a4?? the game would have been a draw) Ka8 15 a4 Kb8 16 a5 Ka8 17 b6 axb6 (if 17…Kb8 then 18 b7) 18 axb6 Kb8 19 b7. **3 Kd5 Bf4 4 Rf2 Be3 5 Rf7+ Kb6** (if either 5…Kb8 or 5…Kd8 White can continue with 6 Kd6) **6 Kd6 Bc5+** (here we deviate from Fine's 6…Bd4, which only provokes White to make a good move, 7 b3) **7 Kd7 Kb5 8 Rf4 b6** (this move had to be played sooner or later since Black cannot prevent further penetration by White's King) **9 Kc7 Be3** (if 9…a5 then 10 a4+ Ka6 11 Kc6 Bg1 12 Rf8 Ka7 13 Kb5 Kb7 14 Rf7+ Kc8 15 Ka6 and Black cannot prevent White from playing Rb7 followed by Rxb6) **10 Re4 Bf2 11 Kb7 a5** (or if 11…Bc5 then 12 b3 Bd6 13 Ra4 a5 14 Rc4 Ba3 15 Rh4 Be7 16 a4+ Kc5 17 Rc4+ Kd5 18 Kxb6) **12 a4+ Kc5 13 b3 Kd5 14 Rf4 Bc5** (if 14…Bd4 then 15 Rxd4+ Kxd4 16 Kxb6) **15 Rf6 Bd4 16 Rxb6**.

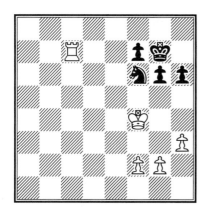

Diagram 172. Szabo versus Trifunovic, Stockholm, 1948. White to move and win.

Answer: White aggressively restricts the movement of Black's Knight and King in conjunction with a Pawn storm. White will also try to provoke Black to advance and weaken his Pawns, while aiming to eventually attack the base of the Black Pawns (currently on "f7"). **1 Ke5 Nh7** (Black has nothing better to do than to make waiting moves, since advancing his Pawns would be weakening and make White's job easier) **2 Rc6 Kf8 3 f4** (White now begins his Pawn storm with the Pawn most likely to spearhead the attack by going to "f5") **Kg7 4 Rd6 Nf8 5 g4 Nh7 6 h4 Nf8** (6…f6+ would allow White's King to penetrate with 7 Ke6 Nf8+ 8 Ke7) **7 f5** (now that he has massed his Pawns, White uses his "f" Pawn to spearhead the breakthrough—the importance of White's pressure on "f6" is becoming more apparent) **gxf5**. Black gets to pick his poison since everything loses. If 7…f6+ then 8 Ke4 Kf7 (if 8…gxf5+ then 9 Kxf5 Nh7 10 Rd7+, or if 8…g5 9 h5 Kf7 10 Rd8 Ke7 11 Rxf8 Kxf8 12 Kd5 Ke7 13 Kc6 Ke8 14 Kd6 Kf7 15 Kd7 Kf8 16 Ke6 Kg7 17 Ke7 followed by 18 Kxf6) 9 Ra6 with the idea of 10 Ra7+. Also, if 7…Nh7 then 8 f6+ Kg8 9 Rd8+ Nf8 10 Kd6 followed by

11 Ke7. **8 gxf5 h5 9 Rd1! Nh7 10 Rg1+ Kh8** (if 10...Kf8 then 11 f6 Ke8 and White can choose his winning method with moves such as the very simple 12 Rg8+ Kd7 13 Rh8 or the more elaborate 12 Rd1 Nf8 13 Kd6!) **11 Kd6.** Black resigned. There is no way of stopping White's King from going to "e7."

We will now examine some of the more advanced endgame checkmates, beginning with how to checkmate with a King and two Bishops against a King and then with a King, Knight, and Bishop against a King. It is impossible to force a checkmate with a King and two Knights against a King (it would only be possible with the cooperation of the opponent). As previously mentioned, the more basic checkmates were covered in my book *Chess for Juniors*.

With a King and two Bishops against a King, White's plan is to drive Black's King to a corner. To reach this goal White's King is centralized and the Bishops are used to cut off Black's escape squares. This mate should take approximately 18 moves with good play on both sides. There are actually numerous ways that the King and Bishops can be used to coordinate the process of driving the King to a corner. However, I will use what I consider to be the easiest and most consistent method for instructional purposes.

Diagram 173. White to move and win.

Answer: 1 Ke2 Kd4 2 Bg2 Ke5 3 Kd3 Kf5 4 Kd4 Ke6 5 Bf3 Kd6 6 Bf4+ Ke6 7 Bg4+ Kf6 8 Kd5 Ke7 9 Bg5+ Kf7 10 Bh5+ Kg7 11 Ke6 Kf8 12 Kf6 Kg8 13 Bf4 Kf8 14 Bd6+ Kg8 15 Kg6 Kh8 16 Bf3 Kg8 17 Bd5+ Kh8 18 Be5++.

I am often asked by my students to teach them how to checkmate with a King, Knight, and Bishop against a King. This checkmate is far more difficult than the previous mate. However, we reach some basic positions that, when pointed out, will help simplify the techniques involved. The first important point to remember is that in order to checkmate the Black King he must eventually be driven to a corner square of the same color as the Bishop. At the beginning White's King and minor pieces are quickly centralized; this will displace Black's King and drive him to the edge of the board. Black will resist by going to the corner of the opposite color of the Bishop. Then the King must be driven from one corner to the other. A major slip could allow Black to escape the net and avoid mate long enough to claim the fifty-move rule, resulting in a draw!

Diagram 174. White to move and win.

Answer: White's King and minor pieces begin their movement toward the center. **1 Ke2 Kd4 2 Be3+ Ke4 3 Nc3+ Ke5 4 Kd3 Kd6 5 Kd4 Kc6** (since it is clear that Black's King is being forced to the edge of the board he avoids heading in the direction of "h8," which is the corner of the same color of the Bishop) **6 Ke5 Kc7 7 Kd5 Kb7 8 Kd6 Ka8 9 Kc6 Kb8 10 Nb5 Ka8 11 Nc7+ Kb8**.

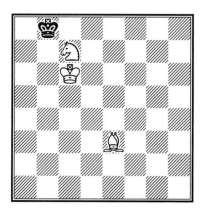

Diagram 175. Position after 11...Kb8.

We have now reached the first important basic position. Black's King is now on the edge of the board and must be driven to the opposite corner (the same color that the

Bishop can attack). White will now lose an important tempo so that the Bishop can gain control of "b8". This will begin to drive Black's King in the direction of "h8". White now begins to use a pattern coordinating all three pieces meticulously to drive Black's King toward "h8". **12 Bc5 Kc8 13 Ba7 Kd8 14 Nd5.**

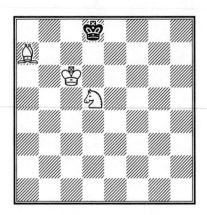

Diagram 176. Position after 14 Nd5.

Here we come to an important juncture. Black has a choice of stubbornly resisting heading toward "h8" with 14…Kc8 (which gives White the easiest time) or trying to outflank White and breakthrough toward the "h1" corner with 14…Ke8 (the best practical chance and Black lives longer).

Variation A: 14…Kc8 15 Ne7+ (White will use a combination of what you might call pulling and pushing Black's King toward "h8" by taking away one square at a time in that direction) **Kd8 16 Kd6 Ke8 17 Ke6** (White keeps Black's King trapped along his first rank) **Kd8 18 Bb6+ Ke8 19 Nf5 Kf8 20 Bc7** (this important tempo loss continues the most simple pattern to drive Black's King to "h8"—however, technically White can achieve his goal one move faster with 20 Be3 Ke8 21 Bg5 Kf8 22 Be7+ Kg8 23 Kf6 Kh7 24 Kf7 Kh8 25 Kg6 Kg8 26 Nh6+ Kh8 27 Bf6++) **Ke8 21 Ng7+ Kf8 22 Kf6 Kg8 23 Kg6 Kf8 24 Bd6+ Kg8 25 Nf5 Kh8 26 Be7 Kg8 27 Nh6+ Kh8 28 Bf6++.**

Variation B: 14…Ke8 15 Kd6 Kf7. Here we have arrived at another important basic position. White must play carefully as Black is trying to make a break toward the "h1" corner by escaping through "g6". **16 Ne7 Kf6** (Black is now trying to break out through "g5") **17 Be3!** (Black's escape squares have been covered and Black's King is contained) **Kf7 18 Bg5 Ke8 19 Ke6 Kd8** (this is as far as Black will get toward "a8") **20 Bf4 Ke8 21 Bc7 Kf8 22 Nf5 Ke8** (note that we have transposed into variation "A"—however, we will still continue with the final moves) **23 Ng7+ Kf8 24 Kf6 Kg8 25 Kg6 Kf8 26 Bd6+ Kg8 27 Nf5 Kh8 28 Be7 Kg8 29 Nh6+ Kh8 30 Bf6++.**

My National Scholastic Champions Prior to 1996

I will begin by giving a little background on the development of the club to which all of my champions have belonged. In 1983 I founded the Chess for Juniors Club in Orange County, California, which moved in 2000 to its new headquarters in Fort Collins, Colorado. I started the club so that my students could receive weekly group lessons and private lessons, attend practice sessions, and play in tournaments.

As the club grew I added weekend training camps, foreign exchange programs, and sophisticated Internet training to encourage students from all over the country to become involved. Prior to the founding of the club I had provided training, mostly in the form of private lessons, to numerous junior students who became strong expert or master players, such as Douglas Root, Roger Poehlmann, and the brothers Andrius and Jonas Kulikauskas.

As a result of starting a formal club I was able to provide my students with the training ground they needed to develop their skills. Within three years of starting the club my students started taking first place honors in championship sections at the National Scholastic Championships. These winners number 35 to date. This doesn't count students such as Walter Shatford and Brent Yamada, who deserve recognition for having scored 7-0 in Junior Varsity sections at Nationals. My club and school teams also became successful. They have won first in championship sections at Nationals ten times.

Below you will find a list of students and the titles they won during the period I was training them. In this and the final chapter I will profile a total of six students, along with at least one game from each player. I will also provide their most current USCF rating, rounded off to the nearest 50. It is nice to see where they stand today.

- RICHARD PHILLIPS (2): 1986 National Junior High (K–8), 1988 National Junior High (K–9).
- ROY RUNAS (2): 1989 National Elementary (K–6), 1990 National Junior High (K–8).
- ASUKA NAKAMURA (3): 1992 National Kindergarten, 1993 National School Grade 1, 1994 National School Grade 2.
- CORY EVANS (2): 1992 National School Grade Kindergarten, 1994 National School Grade 2.
- ANDRANIK MAISSIAN (1): 1992 National School Grade 8.
- RAUL PINOCHET (1): 1992 National School Grade 10.
- STEPHEN KENDRIX (1): 1993 National School Grade K.
- HARUTYUN AKOPYAN (10): 1992 National School Grade 5, 1993 National Elementary (K–5), 1993 National School Grade 6, 1994 National Elementary (K–6), 1994 National School Grade 7, 1995 National Junior High (K–8), 1995 National All America Cup (K–9), 1996 National Junior High (K–9), 1996 National All America Cup (K–12), 1997 National High School (K–12).
- E. J. SCHLOSS (1): 1995 National Kindergarten.
- ALEXANDER HUFF (1): 1995 National School Grade 9.
- JUSTIN SHEEK (2): 1996 National School Grade 9, 1996 National All America Cup (K–9).
- ALEN MELIKADAMYAN (2): 1996 National School Grade 4, 1998 National All America Cup (K–6).
- MINAS NORDANYAN (1): 1996 National All America Cup (K–6).
- MICHAEL CAMBARERI (2): 1999 National All America Cup (K–3), 1999 National School Grade 3.
- STEVEN ZIERK (1): 2001 National Youth Action Championship (K–3).
- SAM GALLER (1): 2002 National Elementary (K–6).
- ANDREW SMITH (1): 2002 National Game/60 (K–12).
- JESSE COHEN (1): 2002 National Youth Action Championship (K–12).

CORY EVANS

Cory Evans (current rating: 2050) started taking private lessons from me and joined Chess for Juniors in January 1992 at the age of four. He had the added benefit of being the son of International Master Larry D. Evans, who is also an excellent chess teacher. Cory started learning how to play chess at 18 months of age and was playing a full game by the age of two!

Cory won the National School Grade Championship Kindergarten section in November 1992 held in Arizona and the Second Grade section in November 1994 held in Florida. Cory's success didn't go unnoticed. He appeared on national television—the *Tonight Show* with Jay Leno and *Inside Edition,* when he gave a 15-board simultaneous exhibition at the Chess for Juniors club. His score was

Cory Evans

12 wins, 1 loss, and 2 draws. As with all the national champions being profiled, he was the subject of numerous newspaper articles.

At age 16 Cory is a sophomore at the University of California San Diego. He is an "A" student with a major in philosophy. His father feels that chess was largely responsible for Cory's great academic success. Cory was known for his aggressive playing style and often used gambit openings. We will now take a look at a game that Cory played when he was only five years old!

Cory Evans versus Dwight Asuncion
Los Angeles, December 1992
Opening: Evans Gambit

1 e4 e5 2 Nf3 Nc6 3 Bc4 Bc5 4 b4

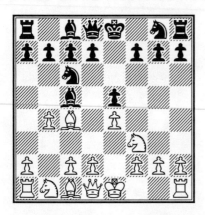

Diagram 177. Position after 4 b4.

Cory initiates the "Evans Gambit." I was asked if this opening was named after Cory or his father. It was actually first used by Captain William D. Evans in the 1820s and shortly thereafter became very popular. It was a favorite of the great American World Champion Paul Morphy during the mid-1800s.

White's idea is to sacrifice his "b" Pawn to gain time to attack in the center with his Pawns. Today theory considers that the gambit does not give White enough compensation for the sacrificed Pawn. However, it is easy for Black to go wrong. Many brilliant games have been won using the Evans Gambit.

4...Bxb4 5 c3 Be7

It would have been slightly better to keep the Bishop more aggressively posted by keeping pressure along the "e1-a5" diagonal with 5...Ba5 6 d4 d6.

6 d4 exd4?

Black should immediately attack White's well-placed Bishop on "c4" with 6...Na5, which might continue 7 Be2 (if 7 Nxe5 Nxc4 8 Nxc4 d5) exd4 8 Qxd4 (if 8 cxd4 then 8...d5) Nf6 9 e5 Nc6 10 Qh4 Nd5 11 Qg3 g6 12 0-0 h5 with about even chances.

7 0-0

Very strong here would have been 7 Qb3 since Black's "f" Pawn is not defendable.

7...Nf6

This active developing move is definitely best for Black. It would have been fatal for Black to go Pawn grabbing with 7...dxc3?? because of 8 Qd5! threatening 9 Qxf7++.

8 cxd4

A good alternative would have been to defend the "e" Pawn with 8 Re1 planning to meet 8...0-0 with 9 e5, or 8...d6 with 9 cxd4.

8...0-0?

Black should have broken up White's Pawn center with either 8...Nxe4 9 d5 Na5 or 8...d5 9 exd5 Nxd5.

9 Nc3?

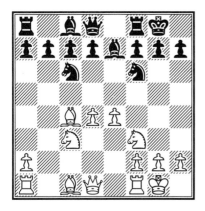

Diagram 178. Position after 9 Nc3.

Stronger would have been 9 e5 planning to meet either 9...Ne4 or 9...Ne8 with 10 d5.

9...d6

Here or on the next move, Black should have played 9...Nxe4 10 Nxe4 d5 to break up White's Pawn center.

10 Be3 Bg4 11 h3 Bxf3?

Black should have maintained the pin with 11...Bh5 instead of giving up the Bishop pair and bringing White's Queen to a more active square. White will now have more than enough compensation for his Pawn due to his nice Pawn center, Bishop pair, and spatial advantage.

12 Qxf3 Nb4?

The Knight becomes a target here. In this difficult position for Black it would have been better to try to reposition his pieces with 12...Nd7 with the idea of 13...Bg5 or 13...Bf6.

13 Rab1

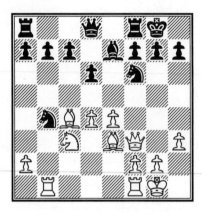

Diagram 179. Position after 13 Rab1.

Cory is quick to take advantage of Black's last move by bringing a Rook onto an open file and pinning Black's Knight.

13...Nc2?

This gives back the Pawn and gives White an overwhelming position. It would have been better to admit that placing the Knight on "b4" was a mistake and play 13...Nc6. It would then be a mistake for White to play 14 Rxb7? because of 14...Na5.

14 Rxb7 Nxe3 15 fxe3 c6 16 e5!

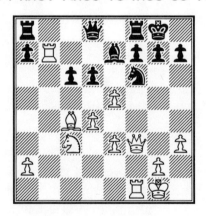

Diagram 180. Position after 16 e5.

Cory deals the crushing blow. This attacks and drives away Black's Knight on "f6" while opening up the "h1-a8" diagonal for White's Queen to attack Black's "c" Pawn.

16...dxe5 17 dxe5 Qd2??

This loses a lot of material without any reason. Black would have lasted longer after 17...Nd7 18 Bxf7+ Kh8 19 Qxc6 Nxe5 20 Qe6.

18 exf6 Qxc3 19 fxe7 Qxc4

Cory was asked what he would have done if Black had played 19...Rfe8?. Cory's answer: 20 Qxf7+ Kh8 21 Qf8+ (21 Qxe8+ also would do the trick!) Rxf8 22 exf8= Q+ Rxf8 23 Rxf8++.

20 exf8=Q+ Rxf8 21 Rxa7 Qe6 22 Rd1 (another nice winning idea is to simplify into an easily won endgame with 22 Qxf7+ Qxf7 23 Rfxf7 Rxf7 24 Rxf7 Kxf7 25 a4) Qg6 23 Rdd7 f6 24 Qxc6 Qe8? 25 Rxg7+ Kh8 27 Rxh7+ Kg8 27 Rag7++.

HARUTYUN ("HARRY") AKOPYAN

Harutyun (known as "Harry"—current rating: 2300) first learned how to play chess in Soviet Armenia where he was enrolled in the Petrosian School at the age of five. He studied chess for two years and then moved to the United States. For a couple of years Harry's parents looked for a chess program suitable for children that would provide him with quality training. In November 1990 I had one of my Armenian students give a large simultaneous exhibition at a school. It attracted both television and newspaper coverage. When Harry's parents saw someone they knew on TV playing against 30 other students simultaneously, and winning all of the games, they quickly tracked me down to enroll Harry.

Harutyun Akopyan

Harry didn't remain rusty for long. Within a couple of months after his training began, he won the Southern California Primary (Grades K–3) Championship. In November 1992 I took Harry to his first National Scholastic Championship. He swept the field winning the Fifth Grade section of the National School Grade Championship with a 6-0 score. This was the beginning of a winning streak with perfect scores at Nationals that lasted for years! Harry went on to win more National Scholastic Championships than any other player at the time when he won his 10th national championship and became National High School Champion in 1997. Harry helped his Chess for Juniors team win the USA versus Germany match held in Hamburg during the summer of 1996. He also represented the United States at the World Junior Championship in Brazil.

Harry had what may best be described as a universal style. His well-rounded style made him equally good at tactical and positional play. He was great at attacking while being resourceful when it was necessary to defend a difficult position. Harry loved playing blitz chess and was comfortable with either slow or fast time controls. Harry's immense love for chess made it easy for him to spend time studying at home and playing in tournaments at every opportunity. These traits were critical factors in making him one of the most successful scholastic tournament players in U.S. history.

One of the most notable features about Harry was that he was a very well liked person. The high level of confidence in his own abilities at chess didn't impact his personality in a negative way. He always showed a high level of respect and kindness toward everyone. I was often involved in raising funds to help Harry travel to major events. Publicity was arranged with front-page coverage in major newspapers and on television. With Harry's talent and great personality, thousands of dollars were donated so that he could compete.

Currently Harry attends Northridge University. He also teaches chess a couple times each week to children at the All America Association Chess Club in Los Angeles.

We will now examine two of Harry's games. In this first game Harry's opponent was known to use the Sicilian Defense. It was the critical last round of the K–5 Section of the National Elementary School Championship. Just before the round Harry and I sat down and reviewed the lines of the Sicilian we felt that his opponent might play. It paid off. His opponent walked right into a line we just reviewed!

Harry Akopyan versus Joshua Wexelbaum
National Elementary School Championship—
Charlotte, North Carolina, April 1993
Opening: Sicilian Defense

1 e4 c5 2 f4

This move, known as the Grand Prix Attack, was Harry's favorite way of playing against the Sicilian. It is an aggressive alternative to playing the usual 2 Nf3 and many players who use the Sicilian neglect to study it.

2...Nc6 3 Nf3 g6 4 Bb5 Bg7 5 Bxc6

White doesn't mind giving up the Bishop pair to double Black's Pawns. White also avoids the variations where Black posts his Knight on "d4".

5...bxc6

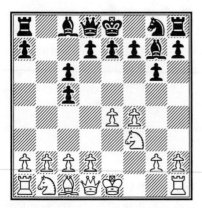

Diagram 181. Position after 5...bxc6.

Black decides to capture toward the center. Also playable was 5...dxc6, which might continue 6 d3 Bg4 7 Nbd2 Nf6 8 0-0 0-0 9 Qe1 with a slight edge for White.

6 Nc3

A good alternative was to play 6 d3 keeping open the option of playing 7 Nbd2.

6...Nf6 7 0-0 0-0 8 d3 Rb8 9 Qe1!

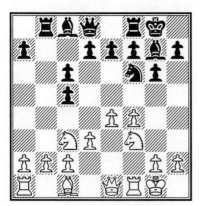

Diagram 182. Position after 9 Qe1.

Harry had two ideas in mind behind this move. First, it prepares to bring the Queen to "g3" or "h4" to assist with the build-up on the Kingside. Second, White would like to move his Pawn to "b3" to block Black's Rook on the "b" file, hinder Black from moving a Pawn to "c4", and allow for the possible fianchetto of a Bishop to "b2". To immediately play 9 b3? would allow 9...Nxe4!. Therefore, the Queen on "e1" will be defending the Knight on "c3" when White moves his Pawn to "b3".

9...d6 10 b3 Nd7?

Black's idea is to prepare support for a counter in the center with his "e" Pawn. However, this move removes the Knight from a superior location. Black would have done better to complete his minor piece development with 10...Bg4.

11 Bb2 e5 12 f5?

Harry is a bit overeager with his attack and releases the tension in the center too early. A simple and good alternative would have been 12 Ne2 defending the "f" Pawn, bringing the Knight toward the Kingside, and opening the "a1-h8" diagonal for the Bishop on "b2".

12...Nb6?

Black's Knight is further removed from being of assistance on the Kingside. Black should have brought the Knight back to assist on the Kingside with 12...Nf6.

13 Qg3

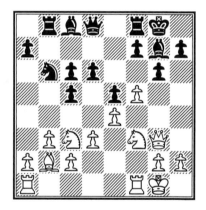

Diagram 183. Position after 13 Qg3.

White continues building up on the Kingside. When first analyzing this position I considered 13 a4 to meet 13...c4? with 14 a5. However, when looking deeper at the line played it became clear that it was okay to allow Black to eliminate his doubled Pawns after 13 Qg3 c4 14 dxc4 Nxc4 15 Bc1 Nb6 16 Be3 because White has a clear advantage.

13...gxf5

This opens up Black's Kingside where he is castled. It would have been better to maneuver his Knight back toward the Kingside, where it belonged in the first place, with 13...Nd7.

14 exf5 Bxf5?

Black should have blockaded the White "f" Pawn with 14…f6. After 15 Ne4 Black then has the choice of playing it safe with 15…Qe7 or winning a Pawn with 15…Bxf5 16 Nh4 Be6 17 Nf5 Bxf5 18 Rxf5. White will still have more than enough compensation for the sacrificed Pawn. After the move played in the game Harry will take quick advantage of Black's exposed Bishop on "f5" and obtain an overwhelming position.

15 Nxe5 dxe5 16 Rxf5 f6

Black defends his "e" Pawn and occupies "f6" before White's Knight can get there.

17 Ne4?

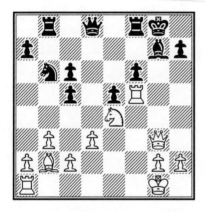

Diagram 184. Position after 17 Ne4.

This move, which centralizes White's Knight and attacks Black's weak Pawns on "c5" and "f6", is actually inaccurate. White should have continued his build-up by first playing 17 Raf1 with the idea of 18 Ne4. The reasoning behind this will be pointed out after Black's next move.

17…Nd7?

Black missed a great defensive resource. He should have played 17…Na4!, which would have greatly minimized White's advantage. After 17…Na4! White cannot play 18 Bc1? or 18 Ba3? because of 18…Qd4+ forking the King and Rook on "a1". Therefore, after 17...Na4! White would do best to continue with 18 Bxe5 fxe5 19 Rxf8+ Kxf8 20 Rf1+ Kg8 21 bxa4. It becomes clear now why White should have moved his Rook to "f1" instead of his Knight to "e4" on the previous move.

18 Raf1 Kh8 19 Qh4

This increases pressure on Black's weak Pawn on "f6" and will soon take advantage of Black's weak Pawn on "h7".

19...Qe7 20 Rh5 h6 21 Bc1!

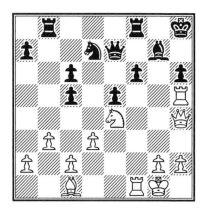

Diagram 185. Position after 21 Bc1.

Sometimes a move that retreats a piece is actually an attacking move! All of White's pieces are now aiming in the direction of Black's King. Black is defenseless against the impending invasion!

21...Rf7 22 Bxh6 Bxh6 23 Rxh6+ Rh7 24 Nxf6 Nxf6 25 Rfxf6 Rb7 26 Rxh7+ Qxh7 27 Rf8+ Kg7 28 Qf6++.

This was a nice victory to clinch Harry's first National Elementary School Championship title.

Jan Pohl (Wichern-Schule team, Germany) versus Harry Akopyan (Chess for Juniors team, USA)
Hamburg, Germany, July 1996
Opening: King's Gambit

1 e4 e5 2 f4

The King's Gambit is not popular today at the Master level. However, it is important to be well prepared for less commonly used openings. Just because an opening isn't used very often doesn't make it inferior. Former World Champion Boris Spassky often used the King's Gambit during the 1960s and 1970s.

White sacrifices his "f" Pawn to remove Black's important Pawn from "e5". This will make it easier for White to occupy the center by placing a Pawn on "d4". White's major plans are to get play on the half open "f" file after castling Kingside and make Black's Pawn on "f4" a target for the Bishop on the "c1-h6" diagonal.

2...exf4

If Black wants to try to get an advantage out of this opening it is best to accept the Gambit. The King's Gambit Declined results in approximate equality after 2...Bc5 3 Nf3 (not 3 fxe5?? because of 3...Qh4+ and now if 4 g3 Qxe4+ forking King and Rook, or if 4 Ke2?? then 4...Qxe4++) d6 4 Nc3 Nf6 5 Bc4 Nc6 6 d3.

3 Nf3 d6

Black immediately contests control of the important "e5" square while freeing his Bishop on the "h3-c8" diagonal. Harry was well versed on this line, known as *"Fischer's Defense."* The former World Champion from the United States, Bobby Fischer, popularized this variation during the 1960s in an article he titled *A Bust to the King's Gambit.* Though not entirely a refutation to the King's Gambit, it is one of the strongest variations for Black.

4 d4 g5 5 Nc3?

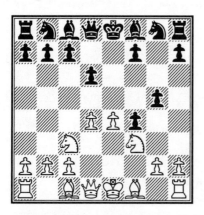

Diagram 186. Position after 5 Nc3.

White has no time for this slow developing move that prevents the possibility of the Pawn going to "c3". Better was one of the main lines with either 5 Bc4 h6 6 0-0 Bg7 7 c3 Nc6 or 5 h4 g4 6 Ng1 f3 7 gxf3 Be7.

5...Bg7 6 Bc4 Nc6 7 0-0 h6 8 Qd3 Nge7

White has not used one of the thematic attacks against Black's Pawn chain by placing a Pawn on "g3" or "h4". Since Harry has a solid position and is a Pawn ahead he keeps the game closed and continues with normal developing moves. He preferred this method, rather than complicating matters and opening up the game with 8...g4 9 Ne1 Bxd4+ 10 Kh1 f3 11 gxf3 Bg7. Black stands better in either case.

9 Re1?

White moves his Rook from a superior file and takes away the "e1" square as a retreat for White's Knight on "f3". White hopes to support the advance of his "e" Pawn. It would have been better to reinforce his "d" Pawn with 9 Ne2.

9...Bg4?

Here it was clearly better to drive White's Knight away from the protection of his "d" Pawn with 9...g4 and if 10 Nd2 then either 10...Bxd4+ or 10...Nb4 11 Bxf7+ Kf8 is good. Here the *"retained image"* probably played a role in both sides not visualizing the "e1" square as no longer available for the retreat of the Knight.

10 e5?

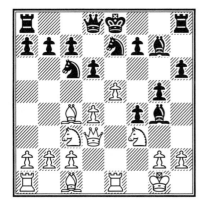

Diagram 187. Position after 10 e5.

This opens the game favorably for Black. The theme of the King's Gambit is to open lines to obtain compensation for the sacrificed Pawn. With the thematic attacks using his "g" and "h" Pawn no longer effective, White unsoundly tosses the "e" Pawn into the fray. It would have been better to play 10 Ne2 or 10 d5 to relieve the pressure on his "d" Pawn.

10...Bxf3 11 gxf3

Harry would have met 11 Qxf3 with 11...dxe5 12 d5 (not 12 dxe5?? because of 12...Qd4+) Nd4.

11...dxe5 12 dxe5

Here 12 d5 would have prolonged the battle. Black's best reply would have then been 12...Na5 with a solid two Pawn advantage.

12...Nxe5 13 Qe4 0-0 (even faster was 13...f5 14 Qxb7 Rb8 15 Qxa7 Nxf3+) **14 Bb3 Re8 15 Kg2 c6 16 Ne2** (16 Rd1 would have prolonged the agony) **N7g6 17 Qb4 Nh4+ 18 Kf2 Nexf3 19 Rh1 a5 20 Qc4 Kh8** (20...Ne5 was more to the point) **21 Ng1 Qd4+** (or 21...Qb6+ forcing a quick mate) **22 Qxd4 Bxd4+** and White resigned.

ALEX HUFF

Alex (current rating: 2100) learned how to play chess at the age of five. Alex and his parents first thought of chess as being like other board games, such as monopoly or checkers, until they discovered the world of organized chess. When his mother found that there was a formal chess club for kids with actual instruction, she brought eight-year-old Alex to give the club a try. Little did she know that this would lead to Alex becoming a national champion! As with all of my national champions, it couldn't have happened without parental support. Alex's father, David, became engrossed with supporting not only his son Alex but also his son's club and chess in general. David made sure that Alex had the opportunity to attend every important chess event. Soon Alex

Alex Huff

was off to all of the major Nationals and team events. David, owner of Good Samaritan Hospital in Bakersfield, California, ended up donating more than $15,000 over the years to Chess for Juniors to help out other kids in chess. Today Alex's father is a major driving force in Southern California scholastic chess as an organizer.

Alex was part of an awesome team that consisted of Harry Akopyan, Justin Sheek, and Justin Skliar, who were all within about a year of the same age and all with ratings between 1800 and 2200. In the mid 1990s they defeated Frank Behrhorst's Wichern-Schule Team in matches in Hamburg, Germany, and Huntington Beach, California. They won the All America Cup (known as the National Game/30 Scholastic Action Championships) and at one national championship had a 1st, 2nd, and 3rd place individual finish in the same section! Alex's major individual achievements in chess include winning the Ninth Grade section of the National School Grade Championships in December 1995 and twice winning the California State High School Championship.

Alex was a newsmaker; he was featured in major newspaper articles and he had a feature story in *Boys Life* magazine in December 1997. Alex was very well rounded. He not only was an excellent student in school but also received top honors in athletics for both soccer and basketball on a regional level (being named most valuable player on his team and in the league).

Alex was an extremely hard worker. He would spend an average of 45 minutes a day studying chess, take two-hour weekly lessons, and play in tournaments a couple of times each month. Alex had a quiet, nonabrasive personality that allowed him to make friends easily.

Alex attended college and then was accepted into the U.S. Army Airborne Chemical Weapons Division in Germany. His two younger sisters, Mimi and Kali, currently take a two-hour Internet lesson from me each week and have done very well in their age group on the state and national level. We will now take a look at one of Alex's games.

Tobias Sosside (Wichern-Schule team, Germany) versus Alex Huff (Chess for Juniors team, USA)
Hamburg, Germany, July 1996
Opening: Queen's Indian Defense

1 c4 Nf6 2 Nc3 e6 3 a3 b6 4 Nf3 Bb7 5 e3 d5 6 d4

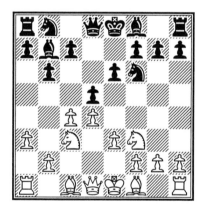

Diagram 188. Position after 6 d4.

This game has transposed from an English Opening into the Queen's Indian Defense. Alex was well versed on the importance of transposing into openings that he knew.

6...Bd6 7 Bd3 0-0 8 0-0 Nbd7 9 Re1

Black will demonstrate that White's plan of using the Rook to support the advance of his "e" Pawn is flawed. Better for White was 9 cxd5 exd5 10 Qc2 threatening 11 Nb5.

9...Ne4

Alex posts his Knight on an active outpost and blockades White's "e" Pawn.

10 Nd2?

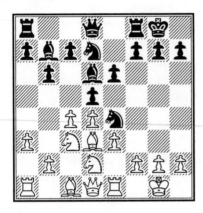

Diagram 189. Position after 10 Nd2.

This removes an important defender from the Kingside and allows Black's coming sacrifice. It would have been better for White to increase pressure on "e4" and activate his Queen with 10 Qc2.

10...Bxh2+! 11 Kf1

It would have been the lesser of two evils to accept the sacrifice with 11 Kxh2 Nxf2 12 Bxh7+ (if 12 Qe2 then 12...Nxd3 planning to meet 13 Qxd3 with 13...Qh4+ forking the King and Rook) Kxh7 with one possible continuation being 13 Qh5+ Kg8 14 Rf1 Nf6 15 Qf3 N2g4+ 16 Kg1 and White has limited his loss to only a Pawn.

11...Nxd2+

It would have been stronger for Alex to bring his Queen into the attack with 11...Qh4.

12 Bxd2 Nf6?

Here Black should have opened up the "h1-a8" diagonal for his Bishop with 12...dxc4 with the possible continuation 13 Bxh7+ (if 13 Bxc4 then 13...Qh4 is strong) Kxh7 14 Qh5+ Kg8 14 Qxh2 c5.

13 cxd5!

White closes off the "h1-a8" diagonal for Black's Bishop.

13...exd5 14 g3

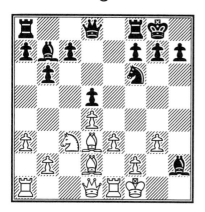

Diagram 190. Position after 14 g3.

White blocks the retreat of Black's Bishop on "h2". Black must be resourceful to avoid losing the Bishop.

14...Bc8!

Alex finds the right plan! Since the Bishop was now shut off on the "h1-a8" diagonal, it is repositioned on a new diagonal, taking advantage of White's weaknesses on the Kingside white squares.

15 Kg2 Qd7!

Black follows through on the only plan that could save him.

16 Kxh2 Qh3+ 17 Kg1 Ng4

Black threatens 18...Qh2+ 19 Kf1 Qxf2++.

18 Qf3 Qh2+ 19 Kf1 Nh6?

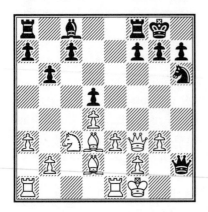

Diagram 191. Position after 19…Nh6.

This is too slow. Perhaps Alex wanted to take his chances and didn't want the draw that would have resulted after 19…Nxf2 20 Qxf2 Bh3+ 21 Ke2 Bg4+ 22 Kf1 Qh1+ (or 22…Bh3+) 23 Qg1 Qf3+ 24 Qf2 Qh1+.

20 Qxd5?

White missed his opportunity to play 20 Ke2! Bg4 21 Rh1! Bxf3+ (if 21…Qg2 then 22 Qxg4! Nxg4 23 Bxh7+ Kh8 24 Be4+ Qxh1 25 Rxh1+ Nh6 26 Nxd5) 22 Kxf3 Qxh1 23 Rxh1 and White's two Bishops and superior position against Black's Rook and Pawn give him a substantial advantage.

20…Bh3+ 21 Ke2 Bg4+ 22 Kf1 Rad8 23 Qb7 Bc8 24 Bxh7+

White's idea is to return his extra material to open up the "d3" square as a possible escape for his King.

24…Kxh7 25 Qe4+ Bf5 26 Qb7?

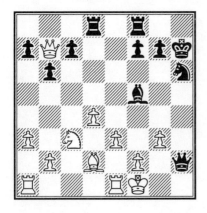

Diagram 192. Position after 26 Qb7.

White should have used his Queen actively to defend on the Kingside with 26 Qh4, which might have continued 26...Bd3+ 27 Ne2 Qxh4 28 gxh4 Nf5 with about even chances.

26...Bh3+

This should have allowed the King to escape. Black had a very neat and subtle winning move. Alex could have played 26...Bg4! preventing the King from escaping on "e2". Black's winning plan would consist of moving his Rook to "d6" threatening either to cut off Black's Queen by placing a Pawn on "c6" (allowing Bf3) or to shift the Rook to "f6" threatening mate on "f2". After 26...Bg4 if 27 Nb5 (to prevent 27...Rd6) then 27...Qh5! with the idea of 28...Bf3 and 29...Qh1++.

27 Ke2 Bg4+ 28 Kf1?

White's King needed to escape with 28 Kd3.

28...Nf5

Black threatens 29...Nxg3+ 30 fxg3 Bh3+ 31 Qg2 Qxg2++.

29 Qe4 Qh5?

Black had the brilliant 29...Rxd4!! 30 exd4 Re8!, and if 31 Qxe8 then 31...Qh1++.

30 Kg1?

This is obviously a simple oversight. White misses his chance to stay in the game with 30 Kg2, which would have left Black with only a moderate advantage after 30...Qh3+ 31 Kg1 c5.

30...Bf3

Black threatens both 31...Bxe4 and 31...Qh1++. White resigned.

chapter 8

My National Scholastic Champions after 1996

MICHAEL CAMBARERI

I remember back in early October 1997 receiving an interesting phone call. A mother from Boise, Idaho had just spoken to her friend who attended my National Scholastic Chess Teachers' Conference in Huntington Beach, California. She wanted me to train her six-year-old son who, she felt, showed a lot of talent. She also wanted my opinion on Michael's ability. At that time I didn't use the Internet for lessons, so I asked, *"How is this possible with you being in Idaho?"* Michael's mother said, *"We will fly out monthly for lessons and to attend your tournaments."* So just before his seventh birthday Michael had his first lesson at my studio.

I was told that Michael was medicated and had ADHD. I was warned that sometimes his feet would be higher than his head when he sat down. Because Michael had so much love for playing chess he was very much in tune with his lessons and did a great job of focusing on them. He also put in the time to study openings and tactics.

Michael started traveling to major scholastic tournaments around the country and attended matches with the club in Montreal, Canada, and Hamburg, Germany. His mother, Kathleen, would always travel with us and assist with the arrangements. In 2000 Michael started taking Internet lessons twice a week. He also loved giving simultaneous exhibitions from which he received great newspaper coverage.

Within two years after Michael started his training with me he started winning first place at numerous National Championships. He won the All America Cup (K–3 Section) held in Arizona in November, 1999 and the Third Grade section of National School Grade Championships held in Kentucky in December 1999. His roll didn't stop there, as he went on to win the K–5 Section of the National Elementary in

Michael Cambareri

Michael Cambareri gives a simultaneous exhibition at the Chess for Juniors Club.

2001 and the K–8 Section of the National Junior High (while in 6th grade) in 2002. Michael is very much a team player. When he moved to Spokane, Washington, he spearheaded his team at St. George's School at both the state and national championships.

Michael Cambareri (current rating: 1850) is an excellent student in school and participates in math competitions. He has a lively personality and is well liked. It might be said that he doesn't have a mean bone in his body. Both his older brother, Johnny, and younger sister, Morgan, play in tournaments, and his parents are involved in organizing scholastic chess in eastern Washington. Now let's take a look at one of Michael's games.

Michael Cambareri versus Phillip Weyland
Spokane, Washington, June 1999
Opening: Petroff's Defense

1 e4 e5 2 Nf3 Nf6 3 d4

This move initiates the Steinitz variation. It is an excellent alternative to the main line, which would have been 3 Nxe5 d6 4 Nf3 Nxe4 5 d4.

3...exd4

Also playable is 3...Nxe4, with one possible continuation being 4 Bd3 d5 5 Nxe5 Bd6 6 0-0 0-0 7 Nd2 Bxe5 8 dxe5 Nc5 9 Nb3 Nxd3 10 Qxd3 Nc6 and now either 11 Bf4 or 11 Qg3 gives White the better game.

4 e5 Ng8?

Michael says *"undeveloping, 4...Ne4 is book."* Michael is absolutely correct and knows that rarely in the opening is it good to retreat a piece back to where it started.

After the correct book move, 4...Ne4, a possible continuation would be 5 Qxd4 d5 6 exd6 Nxd6 7 Nc3 Nc6 8 Qf4 g6 9 Bd3 Bg7 10 Be3 Be6 11 0-0-0 Qf6 12 Qa4 and White is slightly better.

5 Nxd4

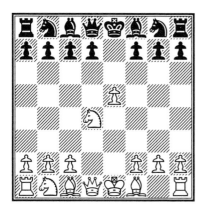

Diagram 193. Position after 5 Nxd4.

White recovers his Pawn and posts his Knight in the center. A good alternative would have been 5 Qxd4 planning to meet 5…Nc6 with 6 Qe4.

5…Bb4+?

As Michael puts it, *"White gets 6 c3 for free."* The result is a loss of time after the Bishop is attacked and driven back. It would have been better for Black to have attacked White's "e" Pawn and free his Bishop on "c8" with 5…d6.

6 c3 Bc5 7 Bc4

Provoking Black to weaken the dark squares on the Kingside with 7 Qg4 g6 8 Qe2 was stronger.

7…d6

Michael correctly stated, *"7…d5 is more forcing."*

8 exd6 Bxd6

It would have been more logical to continue bringing out new pieces with 8…Qxd6 instead of making this retreat with the Bishop. Michael says this move *"moves the Bishop a third time."*

9 0-0 Nf6

Blocking White's attack along the "e" file with 9…Ne7 would have been better.

10 Re1 + Be7 11 Qe2

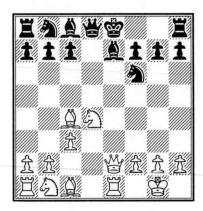

Diagram 194. Position after 11 Qe2.

White increases pressure on Black's pinned Bishop by piling up on the "e" file and preventing Black from castling.

11 ... Bd7

This would be a case where provoking White to move his Pawn to "f3" would have been Black's best idea by playing 11...Bg4 12 f3 Bd7. Having a Pawn on "f3" would have obstructed White from bringing his Queen into play on the Kingside along the "d1-h5" diagonal and would have created more of a weakness by being on "f3" instead of "f2". Since Black wants his Bishop on "d7" anyway, this makes sense.

12 Bf4 Bc6?

The Bishop no longer covers the important "f5" square from "c6", which gave White an awesome opportunity to knock Black out quickly.

Michael says, *"12...Nc6! with the idea of trading off White's good Knight is by far the best plan."* This would follow the principle of making even exchanges of pieces to relieve pressure in a cramped or inferior position. After 12...Nc6 the game might continue 13 Nxc6 Bxc6 14 Na3!. In this case placing the Knight on the edge of the board is an exception to the general rule that I tell to my students, *"a Knight on the rim is dim; its chances are very slim."* After 14 Na3 White's plan is to play moves like Rad1 (attacking Black's Queen) and Nb5 (bringing the Knight into play as a second attacker on Black's "c" Pawn).

13 Nd2?

Michael pointed out himself, *"13 Nf5! forcing 13...Be4 (or 13...0-0 14 Qxe7) 14 Nxe7 Qxe7 15 Nd2"* would have been crushing.

13...a6?

This move was a total waste of time. Michael says, *"13...Kf8 followed by 14...Bd6 is Black's only hope."*

Yes, under the circumstances 13...Kf8, removing the pin from the Bishop on "e7" was Black's best move, which might have continued 14 N2f3 Bxf3 (an immediate 14...Bd6 would be met by 15 Bxd6+ cxd6 16 Ng5! or if 15...Qxd6 then 16 Ng5 Be8 17 Rad1 is overwhelming) 15 Nxf3 Bd6 16 Rad1 with threats of 17 Ng5 and 17 Ne5.

14 Nf5!

White doesn't miss this crushing move when given a second chance! There is no defense to the impending disaster.

14...Ng8

Michael comments, *"horrible, but it's Black's only hope."* Black stubbornly defends his Bishop on "e7" rather than giving it up to get the King into safety with 14...0-0 15 Nxe7+ Kh8 16 Rad1. This would have lasted longer, but would have thrown in the towel right away.

15 Nxg7+ Kf8

If 15...Kd7, White would have a mate in two after 16 Qe6+ (also 16 Be6+ or 16 Qg4+ would do the trick) fxe6 17 Bxe6++.

16 Qh5

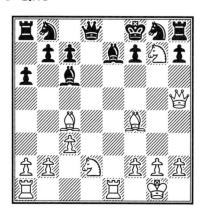

Diagram 195. Position after 16 Qh5.

White brings his Queen directly to the attack on Black's King and threatens 17 Qxf7++. Another nice way to win would have been 16 Ne6+ fxe6 17 Qxe6 (threatening 18 Qf7++) Be8 18 Qh6+ (or 18 Bh6+) Nxh6 19 Bxh6++.

16...Be8

Michael comments, *"not 16...Kxg7 then 17 Qxf7++."*

17 Nxe8

At this point Michael had his pick of nice ways to win. Other choices were either 17 Bh6 Nxh6 18 Qxh6 Kg8 19 Nh5 Bf8 20 Rxe8! Qxe8 (if 20...Qd6 then 21 Qg7++) 21 Nf6++ or 17 Ne6+ fxe6 18 Bh6+ Nxh6 19 Qxh6+ Kg8 (if 20...Kf7 then 21 Bxe6++) 20 Rxe6! (threatening 21 Rg6++) Bf7 21 Rg6+! hxg6 22 Qxg6+ Kf8 23 Qxf7++.

17...Qxe8 18 Bg5

Michael correctly says, *"18 Bh6+ was much better."*

After 18 Bh6+ the game would have come to a quick conclusion after 18...Nxh6 19 Qxh6+ Kg8 20 Re3! Qc6 21 Rg3+ Qg6 22 Rxg6+ hxg6 23 Qxg6+ Kf8 24 Qxf7++.

18...Nc6 19 Re3

The quickest road home was 19 Rxe7! Ncxe7 20 Bh6+ Nxh6 21 Qxh6+ Kg8 22 Ne4 threatening 23 Nf6++.

19...f6?

This allows Michael to finish the game in grand style! Michael is quick to point out that, *"19...h6 followed by 20...Rh7 is Black's only hope."*

After 19...h6 a possible continuation may have been 20 Bf4 Rh7 21 Rae1 Qd7 22 Rg3 (threatening 23 Bxf7! Rxf7 24 Bxh6+) Nd8 23 Ne4 with the idea of 24 Be5 threatening 25 Rxg8+ Kxg8 26 Qg6+ Kf8 27 Qxh7.

20 Bh6+

Michael comments, *"20 Qh6+ Nxh6 21 Bxh6++ is cooler, but it doesn't matter."*

20...Nxh6 21 Qxh6++.

SAM GALLER

Sam Galler (current rating: 1800) from Boulder, Colorado, joined Chess for Juniors in December 1999. Sam was the first local student to join the club when the club moved from California to Fort Collins, Colorado. At the time I started working with Sam he was the Colorado State Elementary School Champion with a rating in the 1100s. Sam's father, Bruce, who was the Colorado State Chess Association's scholastic director, had been looking for a serious chess trainer for some years.

Sam started his training with lessons once a week using a combination of in-person private lessons and Internet lessons. He was a very active tournament player, often playing in two to three tournaments a month. He played on the Chess

Sam Galler

for Juniors team against Germany in Hamburg in 2000 and in the return match in Fort Collins in 2001. Sam gave simultaneous exhibitions, participated in the club's Junior Chess Challenge Exhibits at the local mall, and even started giving lessons to local kids. He was the subject of numerous newspaper and magazine articles. Sam's rating skyrocketed over 600 points in just a little more than two years. When Sam went to the National Elementary School Championship in Portland, Oregon, in April 2002 he was hoping to get a high score and nice trophy. He ended up winning the first place trophy in the K–6 Section and became the first player from Colorado to win one of the major spring nationals (National Elementary, National Junior High, or National High School Championship). In 2003 and 2004 Sam won the Colorado State Junior High School Championship.

Sam is multi-talented. He is one of the top athletes on Summit Middle School's track team, plays tennis, is a straight "A" student, and plays the cello. He won the *Daily Camera*'s regional spelling bee and then went to the Scripps Howard National Championships.

Everyone considers Sam to be a nice guy chess champion. He is very modest and shows a lot of respect toward others. Sam's playing style is very positional. However, when tactics are called for, he is resourceful.

Sam always has a great sense of humor. In one game at the state championships he was down a piece and losing badly. The game was being displayed live in the analysis room to spectators. However, there was one chance. It would require that his experienced opponent make a horrible blunder. His opponent made just the move Sam was hoping for, allowing a mate in one!

After the game I joked with Sam telling him this: *In his badly lost position Sam called on the great chess genie for help. The genie appeared and said, "Every chess player gets three chess wishes during his chess career, how can I help you?" Sam told the genie that he wanted his opponent, who had only two legal moves possible, to move his King to "c8". The genie looked at the position and said, "You've got to be kidding! No one would make such a move that would allow a mate in one." Sam said, "Please! Please! I really want this wish!" So the genie said, "Well, here is what I can do. For such a miracle it will require you to use up all three of your wishes." Sam immediately agreed and poof! The move was made and Sam was saved!*

In the last round game of that tournament Sam needed only a draw for clear first place. In that game a dead drawn endgame was reached and a draw agreed. I asked Sam why he didn't play on a little longer against his lower-rated opponent. Sam told me, *"I have already used my three wishes and now the genie might be working for my opponent!"* Great answer, though Sam was logical in taking the draw since it clinched first place.

I had just covered the Scotch Game with Sam in our lesson a week before the National Elementary School Championships. And, to our amazement, his opponent walked right into the prepared line and lost a Pawn in a trap we covered! Sam's father and I were able to watch the game from the sidelines. We will now take a look at the game.

Jimmy Simonse versus Sam Galler
National Elementary School Championship—
Portland, Oregon
April 2002
Opening: Scotch Game

1 e4 e5 2 Nf3 Nc6 3 d4 exd4 4 Nxd4 Nf6

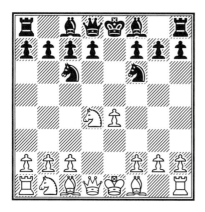

Diagram 196. Position after 4…Nf6.

Another equalizing line for Black against the Scotch Game is 4…Bc5, which might continue 5 Be3 (if 5 Nxc6 then equality is reached after 5…Qf6 6 Qd2 dxc6 7 Nc3 Be6 8 Qf4 Qxf4 9 Bxf4 0-0-0 10 Bd3 Ne7 11 Bg3 Ng6 12 f4 Rhe8 13 Ne2 Bg4 14 h3 Bh5 and now best is 15 f5 Bxe2 16 Kxe2 Ne5 but not 15 Bh2 as Black comes out on top after 15…Nh4 16 g4 f5!) Qf6 6 c3 Nge7 7 Bc4 0-0 8 0-0 Ne5 9 Be2 d5 and now if 10 Nd2 then 10…Bb6 11 a4 N5c6 or if 10 f4 then 10…N5c6 11 e5 Qh4.

5 Nxc6

Another common line for White here is 5 Nc3 Bb4 6 Nxc6 bxc6 7 Bd3 d5 8 exd5 cxd5 9 0-0 0-0 10 Bg5 c6 11 Qf3 Bd6 with approximate equality.

5...bxc6 6 e5 Qe7 7 Qe2 Nd5 8 c4 Ba6 9 b3 Qh4

Diagram 197. Position after 9...Qh4.

Sam comments, *"This move was prepared with my coach in a lesson very recently before the game and gives the unsuspecting White player a surprise. Logical moves give Black a very good game, while the best move 10 a3 results in equality for Black. I was excited to finally use it in tournament play, especially for a national championship."*

This is a very aggressive move. It frees Black's Bishop on the "a3-f8" diagonal and it is easy for White to underestimate the Queen's tactical possibilities against "d4", "e4", and "f2".

10 Bb2

In practical play this natural move is very common. However, it is better to prevent Black's Bishop from going to "b4" by playing 10 a3, which might continue 10...Bc5 11 Qf3 (if 11 g3 then 11...Bxf2+! planning to meet 12 Kxf2 with 12...Qd4+ or 12 Qxf2 with 12...Qe4+ forking the King and Rook in either case) Nb6 12 Bb2 Rb8 13 g3 Qe7 14 Bc3 f6 with approximate equality.

10...Bb4+ 11 Nd2

If 11 Kd1 then 11...Nf4 12 Qe4 (if 12 Qf3 then 12...Ne6 is good) 0-0.

11...Nc3 12 Qe3

White most certainly didn't find it appealing to give up his Bishop pair and castle into an open position with 12 Bxc3 Bxc3 13 0-0-0 Qe7.

12...Ne4

Sam comments, *"Threatening 13...Bxd2+ forking the King and Queen."*

13 Bc1?

Sam sums things up well, *"This defends the Knight on d2 but undevelops the Bishop. Better is 13 g3, chasing my Queen from its powerful location."*

With 13 g3 White would have more than enough compensation for his Pawn after 13...Bxd2+ 14 Qxd2 Nxd2 15 gxh4 Nf3+ 16 Ke2 Nxh4 17 Rg1. Therefore, after 13 g3 Black would do better to play 13...Qg4 14 f3 Bxd2+ 15 Qxd2 Qxf3 16 Qg2 Qe3+ 17 Qe2 Qxe2+ 18 Kxe2 f5 19 Ke3 Nc5 with the idea of 20...Ne6 and Black is solid.

13...Bc3

A strong alternative was 13...f5 planning to meet 14 exf6 e.p. with 14...0-0! 15 Bd3 Rae8 16 0-0 Nc5, or if 14 g3 then 14...Qe7 threatening both 15...Qxe5 and 15...Bc5, and, finally, if 14 Qe2 then 14...Qf4 15 a3 Bc3.

14 Rb1

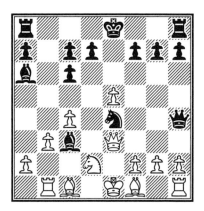

Diagram 198. Position after 14 Rb1.

Sam says, *"Now I win a Pawn by using a combination of threats: If White takes my Knight on his next move then I use the Queen fork on e4 to win material."* Better was 14 g3 Qe7 15 Rb1 Qxe5 16 f4 Qe6 17 Bg2.

14...Nxf2! 15 g3

As Sam previously mentioned, not 15 Qxf2? because of 15...Bxd2+ 16 Bxd2 Qe4+ forking the King and Rook.

15...Bxd2+?

Black should have played 15...Bd4! 16 gxh4 Bxe3 with a clear advantage. The move played in the game will give White a lot more play for the Pawn.

16 Bxd2

It would have been better to activate the King with 16 Kxd2! Qe4 17 Qxe4 Nxe4 18 Ke3. White would have had a lot more pressure for his Pawn.

16...Qe4 17 Qxe4 Nxe4

Sam comments, *"Now Black has a Pawn in exchange for White's space and Bishop pair."*

18 Ba5?

Sam says, *"This does not bother me much after my next move."* This is an awkward post for the Bishop. Better was 18 Bg2 Nxd2 19 Kxd2 and White has a space advantage and active King in return for his Pawn.

18...0-0-0

Black brings his Rook to a more active location, clears the way for a Rook to use the "e" file, and defends his "c" Pawn.

19 Bg2 Nc5?

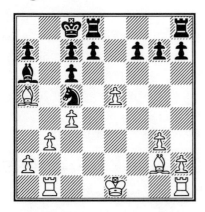

Diagram 199. Position after 19...Nc5.

Black should have attacked Black's weak "e" Pawn with 19...Rde8! planning to meet 20 Bxe4 with 20...Rxe5 (forking the two Bishops and pinning one to the King) 21 0-0 f6. White will end up being a Pawn down without any compensation.

20 Bc3

Stronger was 20 0-0 threatening Black's weak "f" Pawn.

20…Rde8 21 Kd2 Ne6 22 Rhf1 Rhf8 23 Rf2 c5

Sam comments, *"The idea is to trade the boxed-in Bishop for White's good Bishop."*

24 Rbf1 Re7 25 a3 Bb7

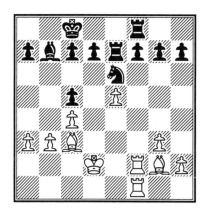

Diagram 200. Position after 25…Bb7.

Black neutralizes White's Bishop on the long "h1-a8" diagonal.

26 Bxb7+?

White exchanges Bishops just like Black wants! White should have kept up the pressure by playing 26 Bd5! offering to trade Bishops on his terms. Then if Black exchanged Bishops with 26…Bxd5 the game might continue 27 cxd5 Nd4 28 Bxd4 cxd4 29 Kd3 Rxe5 30 Rxf7 Rxf7 31 Rxf7 Rxd5 32 Rxg7 h5 and White's more active Rook and King along with the potential outside Pawn will assure him of a draw.

26…Kxb7

Sam comments, *"White's Bishop pair is gone, and I now have to free up my Rooks. White's pressure on f7 does not gain him anything tangible."*

27 b4

Sam states, *"The next move is not best. Better perhaps is 27…d6."*

27…Kc6?

This allows White to expand on the Queenside and results in a loss of time. The idea of having the King play an active role by bringing him to "c6" was good. However, Black should have first played 27…a6 with the idea of 28…Kc6.

28 b5+ Kb7 29 a4 d6

Sam comments, *"I am trying to gain more space, as my Rooks don't have much activity compared to White's."*

30 a5?

White's correct plan was to give Black a backward "d" Pawn with 30 exd6 cxd6 followed by clearing the "d" file for use by his Rooks with 31 Kc2.

30...dxe5 31 a6+ Kc8

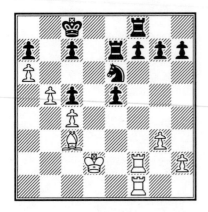

Diagram 201. Position after 31...Kc8.

Now Black will be able to use the open "d" file. The fact that Black has doubled isolated "c" Pawns is of little concern, since he has the potential of making an exchange by moving a Pawn to "c6."

32 Bxe5 f6

Sam says, *"Now my position will improve."*

33 Bb2

The Bishop would have been more actively placed after 33 Bc3.

33...Ng5

Stronger was 33...Rd8+ 34 Kc3 (if 34 Kc1 or 34 Kc2 then 34...c6) Ng5 35 Kc2 Re4.

34 Rf5 Rfe8 35 Rd1

White couldn't play 35 Rxc5?? because of 35...Ne4+. Therefore, 35 Kc1 was better.

35...Re2+

Sam comments, *"The next move is forced, because both Kc3 and Kd3 give me a forced checkmate."*

36 Kc1 Rxh2

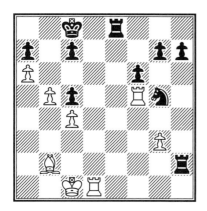

Diagram 202. Position after 36…Rxh2.

Sam comments, *"Taking the Pawn is safe, and makes my Kingside Pawn majority even more dangerous for White."*

However, more dynamic was 36…R8e4 37 Rxc5 Ne6 38 Rc6 Rxh2.

37 Rfd5?

It would have been better to recover a Pawn with 37 Rxc5 planning to meet 37…Ree2 with 38 Bd4.

37…Rg2 38 Ba3 Ne4!

The Knight comes to life with a vengeance! Black is clearly winning at this point.

39 R1d3

White wouldn't stand a chance against Black's three connected passed Pawns after 39 Bxc5 Nxc5 40 Rxc5 Rxg3.

39…Nxg3

Sam comments, *"Now I have three connected passed Pawns that White is not happy with."*

40 Bxc5

Sam comments, *"The next moves will force a trade of Rooks, something that will reduce White's chances of pulling something tricky."*

40…Ne2+

Better was 40…Re1+ 41 Rd1 Ne2+ 42 Kb2 Nd4+! 43 Kc3 (if 43 Kc1 then 43…Rc2+ 44 Kb1 Rxd1++) Rc2+ 44 Kb4 Rxd1.

41 Kb1 Nf4 42 Rd2 Rxd2 43 Rxd2 Kb8

Diagram 203. Position after 43...Kb8.

Sam says, *"Guarding the important "a" Pawn. I now have to watch out for a back-rank checkmate!"*

44 Kc2 h5

This is the first sign that it is the beginning of the end for White. Black's three connected passed Pawns begin their advance.

45 Kd1

The best way to try to stall the advance of Black's passed Pawns was 45 Be3 Ne6 (not 45...Rxe3?? because of 46 Rd8++) 46 Rf2 h4 47 Kd3. However, after 47...Nf8, with the idea of 48...Nd7 and 49...Ne5, Black's Pawns will soon resume their decisive advance.

45...g5 46 Be7 g4!

Sam comments, *"I lose a Pawn but my two passers are more than enough to get a Queen."* Not 46...Rxe7?? because of 47 Rd8++.

47 Bxf6 g3 48 Bd4

Using the Rook actively with 48 Rd7 was better and certainly White's best chance. As a general endgame rule *"it is best to attack passed Pawns from behind."*

48...h4 49 Bg1 h3

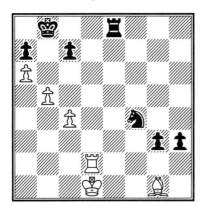

Diagram 204. Position after 49...h3.

Sam says, *"White is dying."*

50 c5 Ne2 51 Rd3 Rh8

Sam correctly states, *"Simply Nxg1 was best."*

52 Kxe2 h2 53 Bd4

White would have lasted longer with 53 Bxh2 gxh2 54 Rd1 h1=Q 55 Rxh1 Rxh1. However, it wouldn't have made a difference.

53...Re8+ 54 Kd2 h1=Q 55 c6 Qe1+ 56 Kc2 Re2+ 57 Kb3 Qb1+ 58 Kc4 Rc2+ 59 Bc3 Qf1 60 Kd4 Qxd3+

Making a point through simplification, this resulted in White quickly resigning. Or simply 60...g2 61 Rg3 Qf4+ does the trick.

61 Kxd3 Rxc3+ 62 Kxc3 g2

White resigned. This game, resulting in the highlight of Sam's chess career, gave Sam the biggest smile for the rest of the evening. The next day Sam, his father, and I spent a relaxing morning at the Portland Zoo (while talking on the cell phone with a couple of reporters).

JESSE COHEN

Jesse Cohen (current rating: 2100) started taking chess seriously when he became my student just before his 14th birthday, in June 2000. I immediately realized that he had both an enormous natural talent and the interest to go along with it. His mother, Arlene, started driving him 40 minutes each way from Longmont, Colorado, for his weekly group lessons. He later added on private Internet lessons and would spend hours each day practicing on the Internet Chess Club.

He immediately got involved in both local and national tournaments, traveling to virtually every major event that Chess for Juniors participated in. He improved rapidly and won the Colorado State Junior

Jesse Cohen

High and High School Championships. He gave simultaneous exhibitions and participated in the Junior Chess Challenge Exhibits at the mall. In the summer of 2002 he traveled to Melbourne, Australia, with the club, where he competed in the Victoria Chess Championship. His successes brought him publicity in local papers, magazines, and even television.

He received national recognition when, in November 2002, he scored 9-0 in the K–12 Section at the National Scholastic Action Championships in Rockford, Illinois. He finished two points ahead of the field! As a result, the Chess for Juniors team won first place in that section, finishing 5½ points ahead of the field!

Jesse is a good student in school, a Black Belt in Karate, and plays the piano. Now we will take a look at a game Jesse played against a local Master.

Jesse Cohen versus James McCarty
Denver, Colorado, May 2003
Opening: Sicilian

1 e4 c5 2 d4

Jesse Cohen says, *"I usually play the Grand Prix Attack with Nc3 or f4 but I wanted to try out a new idea."*

2...cxd4 3 Nf3 Qa5+?

This brings out the Queen early without a constructive purpose. Black should have continued with one of the main lines of the Sicilian with 3...d6, 3...Nc6, or 3...e6.

Jesse comments, *"looks bad because the Queen is out too early and is a possible target."*

4 Nbd2

It would have been better to play a superior version of the Smith-Morra Gambit (where Black's Queen is misplaced) with 4 c3 dxc3 5 Nxc3 Nc6 6 Bc4 where White has more than enough compensation for his sacrificed Pawn.

Jesse comments on his last move, *"hoping to hit the Queen later with Nb3 or Nc4."*

4...Nc6 5 Bc4

Diagram 205. Position after 5 Bc4.

5...b5

This just drives White's Bishop to a more active square where it pins Black's Knight on "c6". Developing with 5...Nf6 was more logical. Jesse says, *"Black should focus on development, not Pawn moves like this."*

6 Bd5

Jesse says, *"I wanted to win my Pawn back."*

6...e6 7 Bxc6 dxc6 8 Nxd4 c5 9 N4f3

Jesse comments, *"I didn't want it to go to b3 because after Qb6 he threatens to trap my Knight with c4."*

9...Bb7 10 0-0 Nf6

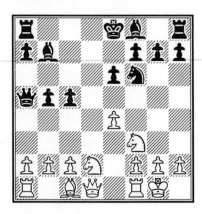

Diagram 206. Position after 10...Nf6.

At this point the position is approximately equal.

11 Qe2 a6 12 a4

Jesse comments, *"I am trying to break down his Pawn structure and open up the file where my Rook and his Queen are lined up. I also have a possible threat of Nb3."*

12...c4

Jesse says, *"This closes down the diagonal from my Queen that was pressuring b5 and prevents Nb3."*

13 e5

Jesse comments, *"This comes in conjunction with the plan of Ne4."*

13...Nd5

Slightly better would have been 13...Nd7 planning to meet 14 Ne4 with 14...b4, expanding on the Queenside and increasing pressure on White's "e" Pawn. Jesse says, *"Better is Nd7 keeping the Bishop's diagonal unblocked and from d7 the Knight can go to c5."*

14 Ne4

Jesse comments, *"continuing with my plan."*

14...Qc7 15 b3?

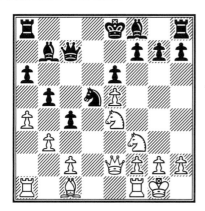

Diagram 207. Position after 15 b3.

This should give Black too much play on the Queenside. White should have exchanged Rooks with 15 axb5 axb5 16 Rxa8+ Bxa8 17 Rd1.

15...b4 16 bxc4

White's best practical chance is to play actively. Therefore, he accepts Black's temporary Pawn sacrifice. After 16 Rd1 Black would have a slight edge after 16...Rc8.

16...Nb6 17 Nd6+ Bxd6 18 exd6 Qxd6?

Black chooses the wrong Pawn. He should have played 18...Qxc4 to meet 19 d7+ with 19...Ke7 (not 19...Kxd7?? because of 20 Ne5+). Black would have had the advantage.

19 a5

Jesse says, *"This keeps the initiative and forces the Knight back to d7."*

19...Nd7 20 Rd1 Qc6 21 Bd2

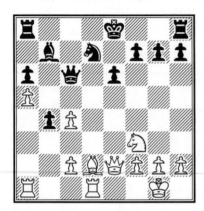

Diagram 208. Position after 21 Bd2.

Jesse comments, *"This is the point of my combo. He is having a hard time guarding this Pawn."*

21...Rc8?

Sometimes the best defense is a good offense! Black missed his opportunity to neutralize White's Queen and equalize the game with 21...Qe4!.

22 Bxb4 Qxc4 23 Qd2

Jesse avoids trading Queens to enhance his attacking chances. White is now threatening 24 Qxd7++ and 24 Qd6. However, the alternative 23 Qxc4 Rxc4 24 Rxd7! Rxb4 (not 24...Kxd7?? because of 25 Ne5+ forking the King and Rook) 25 Ne5 f6 26 Rad1! Bd5 27 Rc7 Kd8 28 Ra7 would also have been good for White.

23...Bd5

If 23...Nf6 then 24 Ne5! Qxc2 25 Qd6 Qc7 26 Qxc7 Rxc7 27 Rab1!. White is threatening 28 Bd6 and Black's extra Pawn doesn't even begin to compensate him for his horrible position.

24 c3

Jesse says, *"This guards my Bishop so I can play Qg5."*

24...Qg4

Jesse comments, *"Preventing Qg5."* Black could have offered more resistance with 24...f6 25 Qe3 Kf7.

25 h3 Qg6 26 Qe3

Jesse says, *"Now I am threatening Rxd5 because of the pin."*

26...Qf5

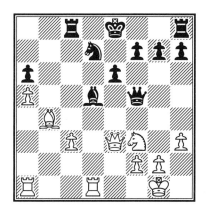

Diagram 209. Position after 26...Qf5.

Jesse comments, *"This guards the Bishop on d5."* If 26...Bc6 (or if 26...Bc4 then 27 Rxd7!) 27 Rxd7! Bxd7 28 Ne5 Qf6 29 Nxd7 Kxd7 30 Rd1+ Ke8 31 Qb6 and Black is dying.

27 Rd4

Jesse says, *"I am slowly increasing the pressure. My next move will be Rad1, doubling on the file."*

A strong alternative was 27 Qa7! (attacking Black's Knight on "d7" and Pawn on "a6") and if 27...Rd8 then 28 Nh4 Qh5 29 Qxa6 planning to meet 29...Qxh4? with 30 Rxd5! exd5? 31 Re1+.

27...f6?

This move loses quickly. Black would have lasted longer after 27...Bxf3 28 Rf4 (if 28 gxf3 then 28...Ne5 is strong) Qd5 29 Rxf3.

28 Rad1 Bxf3?

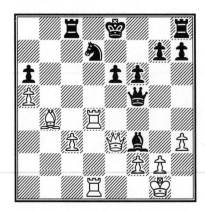

Diagram 210. Position after 28…Bxf3.

Too late! This move should have been played last move. Jesse points out, *"This is a terrible move, which allows a winning combination."*

The best move under these circumstances, 28…Ne5, would have made the game last longer, but the loss would have been painful after 29 Nxe5 Qxe5 (if 29…fxe5 then 30 Rg4 g6 31 Qa7 Qf7 32 Qxa6) 30 Qd3 Kf7 (if 30…Bb7 then 31 Rd8+ Kf7 32 Rd7+ Kg8 33 Rxb7, or if 30…Ra8 then 31 c4) 31 Qxa6.

29 Rxd7! Bxd1 30 Re7+ Kf8

If 30…Kd8, then 31 Qb6+ Rc7 32 Qxc7++.

31 Rc7+

Black resigned. This was the obvious and clear way of demonstrating to White the hopelessness of Black's situation. Since White resigned it was probably Jesse's fastest win in a practical sense, although the move chosen was not the fastest way to win if the opponent played on. The professional will often take the obvious and clearest way to win rather than the fastest way if the latter requires more careful calculation or a degree of risk.

Jesse points out, *"Not the best move but winning nonetheless. Stronger, I found after the game, is 31 Qa7 where mate will follow in about four moves, but I didn't see in the game if Qa7 was so clear and saw that Rc7+ wins immediately, so I went for the clearest win in my eyes."* Smart thinking Jesse!

About the Author

Robert M. Snyder is a highly regarded chess educator and well-known personality in scholastic chess circles. He has introduced chess to more than 170,000 elementary and junior high school students through his presentations. His students have won 35 individual first place titles (a national record) in championship sections at the National Scholastic Championships. His teams have won ten National Scholastic Championship titles.

At the age of 12, Mr. Snyder learned how to play chess. By the time he was 18 he earned the title of National Chess Master. In 1973 he became champion of the Western United States. Mr. Snyder represented the United States on the Correspondence Chess Olympic Team, qualified for the semi-finals of the World Correspondence Championship, and earned an International rating of 2405.

In 1983 he founded the "Chess for Juniors" club, which is now based in Fort Collins, Colorado. He currently trains about 60 local students at the club and about 30 students on the Internet. He has written articles for *Chess Life* and *School Mates* magazines and is the author of *Chess for Juniors, Unbeatable Chess Lessons for Juniors,* and *The Snyder Sicilian*.

EFA; Liquid calcium
ULTRA Body.